How to Talk to Anyone And Everyone

Hold Better Conversation, Master Small Talk And Improve Social Skills

by

MINDNATIC

Mindnatic

PUBLISHED BY: Mindnatic

© Copyright 2022 – All rights reserved.

The content contained within this book may not be reproduced, duplicated or transmitted without direct written permission from the author or the publisher.

Under no circumstances will any blame or legal responsibility be held against the publisher, or author, for any damages, reparation, or monetary loss due to the information contained within this book. Either directly or indirectly.

Legal Notice:

This book is copyright protected. This book is only for personal use. You cannot amend, distribute, sell, use, quote or paraphrase any part, or the content within this book, without the consent of the author or publisher.

Disclaimer Notice:

Please note the information contained within this document is for educational and entertainment purposes only. All effort has been executed to present accurate, up-to-date, and reliable, complete information. No warranties of any kind are declared or implied. Readers acknowledge that the author is not engaging in the rendering of legal, financial, medical or professional advice. The content within this book has been derived from various sources. Please consult a licensed professional before attempting any techniques outlined in this book.

By reading this document, the reader agrees that under no circumstances is the author responsible for any losses, direct or indirect, which are incurred as a result of the use of information contained within this document, including, but not limited to—errors, omissions, or inaccuracies.

Mindnatic

Table of Contents

Your Free Gift — 1

Introduction — 3

Chapter 1: Communication Skills Are a Necessity — 6

Chapter 2: Be Proud of Who You Are — 18

Chapter 3: Approaching Others — 46

Chapter 4: The First Conversation – How to Open It and What to Say — 63

Chapter 5: Your Actions Count Too — 75

Chapter 6: What to Make 'Small Talk' About & How to Keep a Conversation Going — 86

Chapter 7: What Happens When a Conversation Goes Wrong? — 102

Chapter 8: Taking Conversations to the Next Level & Moving Relationships From Superficial to Meaningful — 128

Chapter 9: Tips & Tricks — 151

Discussion — 162

References — 166

Mindnatic

Your Free Gift

You can get instant access to our FREE eBook by signing up to our email newsletter below.

This bonus eBook is 100% free with no strings attached. You don't need to provide any personal information except your email address.

FREE Cheat Sheet:

Be the most CONFIDENT and AUTHENTIC person in the room with these proven techniques!

You will learn:
- √ The Three Pillars of Unshakeable Confidence
- √ The secrets of rock-solid confident people
- √ Steps to building an unshakable confidence
- √ Actionable tips to exercises and consolidate your confidence
- √ and more...

Mindnatic

To get your BONUS

Scan the QR code below

Introduction

There is a quote that says:

"The quality of your communication is the quality of your life." – Anthony Robbins

Does this ring true for you at all?

What did Anthony Robbins mean by this?

Well, as social creatures, we humans desire to connect with and have positive interactions with each other. When we connect with each other in a meaningful way, it satisfies our social needs and makes us feel good. Research has shown that having a strong social network can reduce the negative effects of stress in people, both young and old. On the other hand, loneliness has been linked with depression and chronic health problems.

So the social aspect of our lives is crucial to our well-being, and when it is absent or lacking, it can affect our overall quality of life.

Now, we're going to guess that if you have purchased this book, then your lack of effective communication has gotten to the point where it is starting to impact your quality of life.

Maybe you've always been quieter and more reserved, and communication has never been a problem for you in the past because you've always had people approach you first. For example, you may have always had things like school and sports to connect you with others. But now, as you've gotten older and the opportunities to connect with people over such shared interests have dwindled, you have found yourself in a bit of a communication 'pickle.'

You have come to a point where you've realized that if you want to make any new friends, or you want to ask that attractive person out on a date, or if you want to build your professional network, you desperately need to work on your communication skills. This is a dilemma that is more common than you realize. The number of self-help books on this topic alone tells us that it is a very big and very real problem.

The wonderful thing is that effective communication is indeed a skill—and like any skill, it is one that you can practice and get better at. If you are committed to improving your communication skills and follow all of the tips and suggestions in this book, then you WILL notice improvements in your communication.

Can you imagine how it would feel to:

- Be confident in yourself when you meet new people, whether in your personal life or professional life.

- Be able to know whether someone is interested in talking to you or not.

- Be able to approach someone and just know what to say.

- Be able to make small talk and keep the conversation going.

- Be able to navigate a conversation that goes horribly wrong.

- Be able to move your relationships from surface-level ones to deeper ones.

Well, soon you won't have to imagine anymore, because in this book we will be teaching you exactly how to achieve all these things, and more so that you can take control of your social life once and for all.

Chapter 1

Communication Skills Are a Necessity

"Communication works for those who work at it."
– John Powell

If you have read the first book of our Mindnatic Series, *Detox Your Mind Now*, then you'll know that we stand firmly with John Powell's idea that communication can be learned—*mastered* even—through effort and consistent practice.

Think about any skill you have picked up in your life—whether learning to ride a bicycle or drive a car. Can you recall the steps you needed to take to be able to master that skill? Let's take the classic example of learning to ride a bicycle. First, you probably learned with training wheels. This was a challenge in and of itself because it was something new: you had to learn how to move your legs in a particular motion to make the bicycle move at all, even though the training wheels made it secure. But then came the next step, taking the leap of faith and trying to ride without the training wheels. Maybe your parents were still there to supervise you, which was your security net, but you probably toppled over a few times and grazed your knees before you had mastered riding a bicycle without training wheels.

The point is this: you didn't just go from not knowing how to ride a bicycle at all to having mastered this skill immediately (and if you did, then kudos to you!). It took practice, and this is how it is with communication too. You start with the basics, build up your confidence, and before you know it, you'll have learned how to communicate with ease. It will become second nature, just like riding a bicycle or driving a car.

If you struggle with communication, you can rest assured that good communication simply *does not* come naturally to everyone. Even those super extroverted folk who seem to be natural people magnets have their own shortcomings when it comes to communication.

Think about someone you know or have met who has absolutely no filter, who just says whatever pops into their mind without thinking. This is the kind of person who notices that you've gained a few pounds over the winter and has no problem telling you that you're looking a bit 'chunky' these days.

And think of those people who are extremely opinionated and brash—they will tell you *just* what they think about eating meat, abortion laws, Trump's presidency, and just about anything else, and in a way that screams "it's my way or the highway, and if you think anything different, you're beneath me!"

. . . Or what about those people who do not let anyone get a word in edgeways?

Whether our problem is that we don't talk enough; we talk too much; we don't know what to talk about; or don't know how to express ourselves, *whatever* our unique problem may be, we all have our weaknesses when it comes to communication.

But do you want to know the great news?

The great news is that no matter how 'good' or 'bad' our communication skills are, there is *always* room for improvement. It is powerful to know we are in no way limited by where we are right now in our journey toward better communication.

Given just how important communication is in our everyday lives, isn't it strange that we are never really taught communication skills?

I mean, sure, we go to school and learn the basics—we develop social skills through interacting with our peers and through observing others' behavior. We learn basic manners, like saying please and thank you, and we learn how to share with our friends. We learn how to read and write and how to communicate through language. However, we are never formally taught how to communicate *effectively*.

And suppose you've ever had the misfortune of being rejected or ridiculed by others because of your poor communication skills or lack thereof; in that case, you'll appreciate the value of knowing how to communicate effectively.

Take the story of Sam, for example:

Sam was a typical teenage girl with all of the desires characteristic of a girl her age. She just wanted to feel a sense of belonging and to find acceptance within a group of like-minded young girls. But despite Sam's deep yearning to connect with others, it JUST. NEVER. HAPPENED. Why? Because of the message Sam was putting out into the world, all at a subconscious level. Sam was sending out signals to others that she was disinterested in forming a connection, and she was doing so without even realizing it! You see, because Sam was very shy, she would do things such as sit by herself and turn her face away from others; she would avoid eye contact with others; and when others did approach her or speak to her, she would shut down any conversation by giving short responses and not following up with any questions. Sam was doing everything 'wrong' when it came to effective communication, and it was making others perceive her in the wrong way too! She later found out that because of her avoidant behaviors, others had come to view her as 'aloof,' 'snobby,' and 'self-absorbed' when this couldn't have been further from the truth!

Imagine if Sam had known how to speak to and communicate with others? She could have saved herself years of pain spent feeling lonely and isolated from the people around her. If only she could have held this very book in her hands all those years ago, what a difference it could have made to her life back then!

Effective Communication Makes All the Difference.

Effective communication skills can really be the 'make or break' across thousands of different scenarios.

In our personal lives, we do not only need 'good enough' communication skills to connect with people and make new friends but also to maintain and strengthen our existing relationships. If you do not know how to approach people or build a relationship with someone from the ground up, you could potentially end up very lonely. And if you don't know how to treat others with empathy, and resolve conflict peacefully, then those relationships you worked so hard on developing in the first place won't last very long.

From a professional point of view, we need good communication skills to build business relationships, work effectively in teams, negotiate, accommodate different viewpoints, and more. All things considered, effective versus noneffective communication can make the difference between connecting with others and achieving our communication goals, or not.

So what the heck is *effective* communication all about anyway?

The Four Primary Precursors for Effective Communication

We think four primary components can be considered 'precursors' for effective communication. This means that, without these components in place, communication would be mostly *ineffective*.

Here's a helpful analogy:

Did you know that some vitamins our bodies need are found in the foods we eat in 'precursor' form? For example, carrots contain beta-carotene that is converted to vitamin A only once 'activated' in the body. Only once activated can beta-carotene be transformed in a way that allows it to fulfill its *vital* function of supporting various bodily processes such as vitamin A.

Similarly, we can think about the function of 'effective communication' as being 'activated' when its four 'primary precursors' are working well.

So, what exactly are these 'mysterious' precursors we are talking about here?

Well, let's turn our attention to the diagram below for a moment:

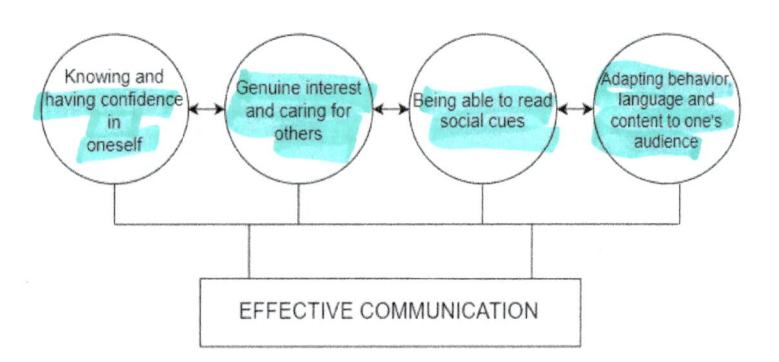

```
┌─────────────┐   ┌─────────────┐   ┌─────────────┐   ┌─────────────┐
│ Knowing and │   │   Genuine   │   │Being able to│   │  Adapting   │
│   having    │◄─►│  interest   │◄─►│  read social│◄─►│  behavior,  │
│ confidence  │   │ and caring  │   │    cues     │   │ language and│
│  in oneself │   │  for others │   │             │   │content to   │
│             │   │             │   │             │   │one's audience│
└──────┬──────┘   └──────┬──────┘   └──────┬──────┘   └──────┬──────┘
       │                 │                 │                 │
       └─────────────────┴────────┬────────┴─────────────────┘
                         ┌────────┴────────┐
                         │ EFFECTIVE COMMUNICATION │
                         └─────────────────┘
```

The four circles represent what we believe are the four 'precursors' for effective communication, namely: knowing and having confidence in oneself; genuine interest and caring for others; being able to read social cues; and adapting behavior, language, and content to one's audience. We believe that without these four essential components working together, effective communication cannot happen.

Let's think back to the story of Sam and examine where Sam may have fallen short on these four 'precursors' to effective communication.

Precursor One: Knowing & Having Confidence in Oneself

Sam was described as someone who was 'shy.' And if we look at the dictionary definition of 'shy,' it refers to a person who is 'hesitant in committing oneself,' 'secluded,' 'hidden,' and 'disposed to avoid a person or thing.' Now, I am not sure what *you* think, but that doesn't sound to me like someone who knows and has confidence in herself (which is our first precursor for effective communication).

Having the characteristic of being shy or being socially anxious can substantially limit people when it comes to communicating effectively. How is someone supposed to practice effective communication skills, like making conversation with others, when they are hyper self-conscious around others, or when they hold very rigid, negative beliefs about themselves?

Note. If shyness and social anxiety are your main concerns when it comes to communicating with others, we would strongly suggest (if you haven't already) addressing these issues first. Make sure to get your hands on our first book in this series, *Detox Your Mind Now,* as well as our CBT workbook if this applies to you. Don't worry. We have priced these books for FREE! Addressing any underlying issues *first* will help set you up for success when it comes to learning and applying the communication skills taught in this book and in our future books to come.

Precursor Two: Genuine Interest & Caring about Others

The next precursor, 'showing genuine interest and caring about others,' is not something that Sam demonstrated either. That is not to say that she *wasn't* interested in others—we know she very deeply *wanted* to connect with people. It's more that she didn't display this desire in her actions. As she was very self-conscious, she was more concerned with her fear of rejection and about things like saying or doing the wrong thing. That is to say, she cared more about herself, specifically how she came across to others.

Precursor Three: Being Able to Read Social Cues

Since Sam lacked self-confidence and was so self-conscious, she did not pick up on social cues—in fact, she was so avoidant that she would not even have paid attention to them. Again, she was more concerned about avoiding social contact and 'protecting' herself from potential rejection, causing her to fall short of the third precursor as well.

Precursor Four: Adapting Behavior, Language & Content to Your Audience

Obviously, because Sam was not 'putting herself out there' and was not exposing herself to interactions with others, she never got to practice precursor four—adapting her behavior, language, and content to her audience.

Like Sam, perhaps you have—until now—in your interactions with others fallen short regarding these four 'precursors' to effective communication. If you have, then don't worry. You're in just the right place!

This book was designed specifically for people just like you, by people who have walked in your shoes.

You can draw a lot of inspiration and encouragement from the fact that we *know* how it feels to be held back in your social life because of poor and, in some cases, what seems like non-existent communication skills. Not only do we share in your experiences, but we have *overcome* many of your struggles. We believe this makes us worthy alliances, bringing you tried and tested tips, hand-picked from our personal experiences, coupled with research-backed insights.

As you make your way through this book, you will progressively learn to master the art of effective communication, such that by the time you turn over the final page, you will feel equipped and confident to go out there and talk to anybody and everybody!

Chapter 1 Key Takeaways:

- ✓ We *all* have weaknesses when it comes to communication.

- ✓ Great communication skills can be *learned*.

- ✓ Communication can be effective or ineffective.

- ✓ There are four primary 'precursors' to effective communication.

- ✓ Knowing and having confidence in oneself; genuine interest and caring for others; being able to read social cues; and adapting behavior, language, and content to one's audience are necessary for *effective* communication.

CHAPTER 2

Be Proud of Who You Are

"Authenticity is the daily practice of letting go of who we think we are supposed to be and embracing who we are."

— Brené Brown

Have you ever tried to change or hide who you really are because you thought others might 'reject' the real you? The need to fit in and belong is our third most important need according to Maslow's hierarchy of needs. This need, which can be classified as a social need, comes right after our most basic needs, like our needs for food, water, shelter, safety, and financial security.

The need to belong and be accepted by others is so ingrained in our human psyche it can lead us to go to some extreme lengths to have it fulfilled. Read about what happened in Matt's case:

When Matt participated in a speed dating event, he became so anxious that the women he met would reject him based on his job, hobbies, and background that he fabricated a life story completely removed from his actual reality. Matt was a successful computer programmer who enjoyed gaming in his free time and came from a small town. His biggest concern with being his authentic self was that if the women knew he was a programmer and a gamer, they would immediately form an image of him as a nerd. He also thought they might think the fact he came from a small town made him a bit 'weird.' So, Matt told the women he met he was a Business Development Manager at a large IT firm, who loved motocross, and who grew up in New York.

We All Wear a Mask to Some Degree

Sometimes, as in Matt's case, because we do not believe who we are is worthy of others' acceptance, we put on a mask and pretend to be someone we are not.

Putting on a mask does not have to look like making up a completely different life story, as in Matt's case. It can also look like holding back and refraining from making any meaningful self-disclosures to others.

That could include anything from hiding what we genuinely like, including our interests and hobbies, to holding back on giving our honest opinions and sharing our true beliefs. It may look like simply agreeing with others in an attempt to appear relatable and make others like us.

No matter how we use it, what does putting on a mask *really* do for us?

Does it *really* keep us safe? Does it *really* win others' acceptance?

Does the Mask Really Protect Us?

For years, researchers have been studying what makes people 'likable' and guess what? Being 'fake' or 'inauthentic' is not high up on the list. In fact, it does not feature whatsoever. What we *do* see up there on the list, among other factors, is 'realness,' the opposite of being 'fake.'

You see, people are quite intuitive, and sooner or later, they will begin to catch on that there's something 'fishy' going on and that you are not who you say you are. When they start to see the inconsistencies in what you say and how you behave, they will start to lose respect for you as they realize you do not have a secure sense of who you are.

On the other hand, if you are someone who is 'real,' who speaks up about what you really think and believe, and who acts in accordance with that, you become someone that people trust because people see you have integrity. People like and trust consistent people, and if you do not know who you are or are always trying to act like someone you are not, this will catch up with you. After all, nobody can keep up an act forever.

Removing the Mask

So, how do we develop the courage to remove the masks we believe have been protecting us but have, in fact, been holding us back from really *connecting* with others?

We can do this by taking the time to reflect on who we really are, by accepting ourselves—'flaws and all'—and by building up our self-confidence.

Doing these things is *crucial* if we want to be able not just to talk to but really *connect* with others in a meaningful way.

In the next part of this chapter, we are going to take you through some practical activities to help you rediscover yourself to promote self-acceptance and build your confidence.

Activity 1. Who Are You?

The first activity we would like you to complete addresses the first point we made about getting to know yourself better to better connect with others.

Remember, it is important to get to know yourself better because without adequate self-knowledge, you run the risk of coming across as 'fake,' whereas if you truly know yourself, you can better express and share who you are with others.

Humans are multi-faceted and complex beings, and we derive our sense of self—our identities—from different aspects of our lives. We construct our identities based on our professions, our interests, our skills, our personality, our spiritual beliefs, and even our closest relationships.

Taking this into consideration, we have created a 'set of questions' of sorts, which covers all of these multidimensional facets of what makes us who we are.

1: Personality

What words would you use to describe yourself?

What would you consider your strengths? If stuck, think about your proudest accomplishment: what strength can you draw from that?

What would you consider your weakness/an area for improvement?

What do others admire about you? If stuck, think about compliments that others may have given you.

Who inspires you and why?

2: Interests/Hobbies

What do you enjoy doing in your spare time? (If you don't do anything now, think to when you were a child—was there anything you did then that you'd still enjoy now/are too busy to enjoy now?)

When was the last time you did something and felt completely absorbed by it?

What kind of books do you like to read? Or what movies/TV series do you like to watch?

What kind of food do you like to eat?

What music do you like?

3: Career/Studies

What kind of work/studies do you do?

Do you enjoy your work/studies? What part do you enjoy most? If you don't enjoy what you do, what would you rather do?

What is your long-term career/study trajectory?

If money were no object, what work would you be doing?

What is the most important thing to you when choosing a career?

4: Family

Are you single/married?

Which relationships do you consider the closest ones in your life at the moment?

What is your family like?

What values did your family instill in you growing up?

Are you happy in your current town/if you could move, what would be your ideal location?

5: Spirituality

What do you believe to be fundamentally true about the world?

Are you religious/spiritual, and what religion/spiritual teachings do you follow?

Do you believe in the afterlife?

What do you believe is your purpose in life?

What or who has influenced your spiritual beliefs?

We would like you to answer these questions and write down your answers in a notebook or on a piece of scrap paper. We encourage you to really take time to reflect on each of the questions before answering.

Hint. If you'd like to make this activity even more fun, you can try it out with a friend or partner. Try asking one another the questions, or even try to guess the one another's answers and see how much you *really* know about one another!

Activity 1.1 – Extension Activity – Creative Self-Expression

Now that you have completed activity one, you should be starting to get a better sense of what makes you unique. Perhaps these things were already in the back of your mind, but perhaps there are some parts of yourself you had 'forgotten' or needed reminding of.

The next step or activity we want you to complete that will help solidify your self-concept, and help you celebrate and be proud of who you are, is a creative one!

We want to encourage you to take what you learned about yourself from activity one and create a collage or piece of art that represents who you are as a person.

You have full artistic license to create your 'artwork' in whatever way you see fit.

If you are stuck or are not really the 'creative' type, then here are some ideas to get you started:

Creating a Collage That Represents and Celebrates WHO YOU ARE

What you will need (materials):

1 x Large colored card

Glue and scissors

A few old magazines

Instructions:

1. Flip through some old magazines and tear/cut out any images or words that resonate with who you are, as you uncovered in activity 1.

2. When you have enough words and images, trim them as needed and arrange them on the large colored card.

3. When you are happy with the arrangement, go ahead and stick the words and images onto the colored card so that you create a 'collage' of everything that represents who you are.

When you have completed the artwork, take some time to

reflect.

Make sure to put your artwork where you can see it regularly: this will act as a reminder to yourself of the wonderful and unique person you are.

If you are feeling brave, you can share your artwork and the meaning behind it with someone close to you.

Activity 2. Exploring Your Values

In the first activity, we explored who you are from the perspective of 'what' makes you, YOU.

We have yet to explore your 'WHY,' which is underpinned by your values.

Now, what do we mean by your WHY? . . . We simply mean what motivates you!

You see, behind all of the decisions we make in life, and behind all of our actions, is motivation: a reason for doing whatever it is that we are doing that holds unique and significant meaning to us.

For example, let's say you decided to become a teacher—WHY

you chose this career says a lot about what you value, about what is important to you in life.

What is fascinating is that the meaning or the *value* underlying your decision could be completely different from what someone else valued when *they* chose teaching as a career.

Maybe you chose to become a teacher because you value making a difference in the world through education: this could fall under the value of 'altruism.' Someone else may have chosen to become a teacher because of the long holidays that teaching offers. For this person, they might value the flexibility that teaching offers.

Knowing WHY things are important to you strengthens your self-concept: if you are firm in what you stand for, others will notice this too. Your self-confidence will shine through, and others will respect you.

Compare the manager who communicates the importance of punctuality to their team when someone pitches up late for a meeting versus the one who only *sometimes* reprimands late employees and other times just lets things 'slide.'

Which of these managers has a clear grip on their values, and which one would you trust and respect more? *We're* going to go with the one that shows more consistency!

While knowing yourself well (that is what makes you, you) will get you through your first meetings and conversations with people, when it comes to 'going the distance' and building real relationships, *knowing* and *communicating* your values is what counts.

So, now that you understand what values *are* and why they are *important*, we're going to introduce you to an activity that is going to help you discover what *your* values are!

Activity 3. Your Top 10 Values

On the next page, we present you with a table—this table includes some 'typical' values held by people. We'd like you to go through this table and make a mark next to all the values that resonate with *you*. It is important when going through the values to go with your 'gut' instinct. If you're unsure, just move on and see if the next value resonates or not.

Then, once you have finished going through the entire table, if you marked more than 10 values, go through the table again and narrow down the values that you chose until you get to your 'top 10.' Then, write them down and reflect on why they are important to you and whether you feel you are living in alignment with them.

Note: If you thought of a value you hold that is not listed in the table below, that is perfectly fine. Feel free to write this or others down as one of your top 10 values.

Values Table

Ambition	Altruism	Achievement	Balance	Calmness
Creativity	Curiosity	Compassion	Challenge	Discipline
Equality	Faith	Family	Freedom	Growth
Gratitude	Goodness	Health	Honesty	Humor
Innovation	Independence	Intelligence	Kindness	Leadership
Loyalty	Money	Openness	Optimism	Passion
Power	Privacy	Reliability	Respect	Security
Simplicity	Stability	Spirituality	Status	Success
Tolerance	Trust	Tradition	Unity	Variety

My top 10 values:

1._____ 6._____

2._____ 7._____

3._____ 8._____

4._____ 9._____

5._____10._____

Reflection Questions:

1. Were you aware of these being your values?

2. Which values were you less aware of having?

3. Are you living in alignment with your values?

4. How might your life be different if you *lived* in line with your values?

Now that you have finished activities 1, 2 and 3, you should start getting much closer to the REAL, authentic you.

That means we can move on and begin to look at how you can build acceptance and confidence in who you are.

Before we begin with that, we'd like to ask you to rate how you feel about yourself. So, on a scale of 1–10, how much would you say you accept yourself as you are right now? (With 1 being 'I do not accept myself at all' and 10 being 'I 100% accept myself'.)

On the same scale of 1–10, how self-confident would you say you are?

If you scored lower than 7 for either self-acceptance or self-confidence, we'd suggest—if you haven't already—to go back and read the first book in this series, *Detox Your Mind Now*, as well as our CBT workbook, as these tackle self-esteem issues from a much deeper level. This book, combined with our CBT workbook, can help you combat more rigid negative beliefs you may hold about yourself. Sometimes our level of self-confidence can shift a little depending on our mood. So think about whether you are simply having a bad day and your confidence is lower than normal, or if your confidence being lower than normal is something more permanent.

The strategies we are going to teach here to promote self-acceptance and self-confidence do not address the root of your problems. They are just meant to give you a slight boost in the right direction. These activities work best if practiced regularly and made part of your daily routine versus just being practiced once-off.

3.1 Promoting Self-Acceptance

Many people who struggle with communication have an underlying fear of being rejected and judged by others. Often, but not always, they may have had negative experiences around communicating with others in the past. Perhaps they were bullied at school, maybe they were a bit different from others, or maybe they did very poorly when it came to public speaking.

Whatever the case, people who struggle with communication typically have some underlying fear that holds them back from engaging with others in the ways they would like to.

This fear, combined with *desperately* wanting to be better communicators, can put a lot of pressure on people and cause them to become hyper-critical. This lack of 'self-acceptance' and focus on what is 'wrong' or what 'could' go wrong is what leads to such issues as social anxiety.

So, what is the solution?

Well, how about we focus on treating ourselves with compassion and manifest self-acceptance instead of setting such high expectations for ourselves and judging ourselves so harshly?

This is exactly what we are going to teach you in the next activity, which is a strategy borrowed from 'Acceptance and Commitment Therapy.' It focuses on *accepting* our negative emotions, being *kind* and *compassionate* toward ourselves and *moving toward* behaviors we *value*.

Activity 4. Radical Acceptance

Radical acceptance is the practice of accepting situations for what they are, accepting what you cannot change, and showing kindness and acceptance toward yourself.

So, how exactly do we go about practicing radical acceptance? Here are some steps:

1. Think of an event in your life you have had a hard time accepting (it could be something recent or something from the past).

For example, perhaps you were bullied at school and have a hard time accepting this and always think about it.

Write down the event you have a hard time accepting:

_____
_____
_____
_____

2. In the next steps, you should think about what 'caused' the event. Think about the facts only, and do not make judgments here. Try to show understanding, kindness, and compassion.

For example, to say you were bullied because you were a 'loser' is a judgment. What are the facts? Perhaps you were a bit different from the other students (which is not a bad thing as being different makes us unique and special in our own ways). Young people are foolish and do not know how to treat others who are different from them. They have not developed high empathy skills and do not realize the impact their bullying can have on others.

Write down what caused the event you have a hard time accepting:

_____

_____

_____

_____

3. Step three is about accepting any feelings you have when thinking about the event, as well as any physiological responses you feel in your body.

For example, perhaps you feel really angry that the bullies treated you the way they did, and maybe you also feel a sense of sadness. Maybe your heart rate increases, and your palms get sweaty when you think about this.

Feel and accept any feelings that come up and remind yourself that you cannot change the past.

Write down any feelings or physiological reactions you have in response to the event:

_____

_____

_____

_____

4. In step 4, we want to create what we call a 'proactive plan.' This is a plan to counter the situation and its impact.

For example, if this experience has led you to now feel awkward and anxious when communicating with new people, what can be done about it?

You may decide you want to feel comfortable and 'okay' with talking to new people. So, you create a plan: the next time you feel anxious, you will accept the feeling and move forward with the conversation. You will try to be realistic and not *assume* that others see you as awkward.

Following these 4 steps encourages 'letting go' of what cannot be controlled by us, seeing reality from a more objective perspective, and treating ourselves with kindness.

Meditation is another great way to enhance self-acceptance, as the aim of meditation is also to 'let go' of thoughts and to learn how not to be controlled by our thoughts. Like with the radical acceptance activity, with meditation, we learn to accept what is and focus only on where we can effect change.

Now that we have tackled how to manifest self-acceptance, let's move on to how you can go about building your self-confidence.

4.1 Promoting Self-Confidence

In activities one and two, you spent a lot of time exploring who you are.

Sometimes, we may not necessarily like who we are—maybe we have been told by society or people around us that some personal qualities are 'better' than others. For example, being very extroverted is something that is exalted in Western societies.

If we have low self-esteem, these kinds of messages can make us seriously doubt ourselves and question our worth.

The truth is, though, (as cliché as it may sound!), we are *all* special and unique in our own ways. Imagine if everybody were the same—what a boring world we would live in!

Remember what we said earlier: people like people who are REAL. So it doesn't matter if you're a little different. What truly matters is that you OWN your differences, that you feel confident in your own skin.

So, how can we go about feeling confident in ourselves?

Well, besides what we teach in *Detox Your Mind Now* and our CBT workbook, another way is through affirmations.

What Are Affirmations?

Affirmations are positive self-statements that we can tell ourselves to remind ourselves of all the great things about ourselves.

Practicing affirmations is easy and just requires you to dedicate 5 to 10 minutes a day to practice saying positive things about yourself, to yourself!

Here are some step-by-step instructions:

Activity 5. Affirmations

1. Go back to the questions you answered in activity one.

Look specifically at what you wrote down about your personality, your strengths, your skills, and your accomplishments.

2. Based on what you wrote down, come up with and write down 10 positive statements about yourself—about the very essence of who you are.

For example, "I am determined," "I am a great singer."

3. Set 5 to 10 minutes aside in your day where you can 'practice' saying these 10 statements to yourself repeatedly.

4. It is best to say these things to yourself while looking at yourself in a mirror—this enhances the experience and feels more sincere when you look at yourself and say the statements out loud, with pride.

1. I am_____ 2. I am_____

3. I am_____ 4. I am_____

5. I am_____ 6. I am_____

7. I am_____ 8. I am_____

9. I am_____ 10. I am_____

In this chapter, we have so far covered three important aspects that can help you cultivate authenticity: knowing yourself, building acceptance, and confidence in yourself. As already discussed, authenticity is important when it comes to effectively communicating with others. People like people who are REAL.

But is that *all* that is needed to make you likable and to have better communication with others? And isn't there a chance that people may not like the REAL you?

What Makes People Likeable Outside of Authenticity?

Well, to answer the first question, likeability isn't just attributed to authenticity. To answer the second question—yes, there is always a chance that others will not like you for who you are. These are very simplified answers to complex questions, so we're going to break this down a bit more.

First, let's look at what ELSE makes someone likable:

Likeability is determined by—as we already know—'authenticity,' but it is also determined by 'empathy,' 'relevance,' and 'friendliness.'

Empathy means the ability to understand others from their own perspective, even if you do not necessarily agree with their logic. This is something we will teach in a later chapter.

'Relevance' refers to how similar two people are or how much 'common ground' they have. For example, if you were chatting in a group of 10 people and someone started talking about something you have an interest in—let's say, running—then you would probably find it easy to jump into this conversation. You would probably also find that having the same interest in running as this other person would help you connect and 'click' with them better because it would be something you can both relate to, and that makes you similar or 'relevant' to one another.

'Friendliness' refers to warmth and openness, which is often communicated through body language and tone of voice. Think about the friendliest person you have ever known. What picture comes to mind? What kind of qualities does that person have, and how do they make you and others feel? You'll probably find they smile a lot, are gentle and kind, and are inclusive—they are always looking for ways to welcome and include others. In a later chapter, we will look at how to communicate that you are friendly.

Now, with the knowledge of what else makes someone likable, let's go back to the question:

'Isn't there a chance that people won't like the real me?'

Well, there's a big difference between showing and being your authentic self in a way that communicates you are above others versus in a way showing respect for your and others' differences. Being able to be yourself while also respecting and showing appreciation for others despite them being different from you (referring to the quality of 'relevance') is the quality of having empathy.

If you have empathy for others, even though there are not many similarities or 'relevance' between the two of you, they will probably still like you. The same goes for friendliness: if you can express warmth and openness to others, whether they share the same beliefs, opinions, and preferences as you or not, you will still be likable. People who have empathy and are friendly are inclusive and welcoming of everyone and are non-judgmental. That is why others are drawn to them. They make others feel comfortable being themselves around them.

So, to be likable, whether you have commonalities with others or not (relevance), empathy and friendliness are crucial.

To summarize what we taught in Chapter 2, it is important to know yourself and have confidence in yourself, as this is what allows you to be authentic with others, and people like authenticity. Being authentic does not mean that others will surely like you, especially if your self-confidence starts to verge on arrogance. The sweet spot is being able to be yourself with others while still respecting others' differences.

Chapter 2 Key Takeaways:

- ✓ Fear of rejection and judgment can hold us back from communicating effectively with others.

- ✓ We fear rejection because somewhere along the line, we learned that we are not valuable.

- ✓ To value ourselves, we need to know ourselves and be reminded of what makes us special and unique.

- ✓ When we know who we are, we can work on building self-acceptance and self-confidence.

- ✓ People like authentic people, but there is always a risk that people will not accept us for who we are.

- ✓ If we can be ourselves and at the same time respect and appreciate others' differences, we will still be likable.

Chapter 3

Approaching Others

"We should approach others openly, recognizing each person as another human being just like ourselves."
— Dalai Lama

The Dalai Lama gave some great advice on approaching others, advice that resounds with what was proposed by our second 'precursor' to effective communication: genuine care for and interest in others. Jesus of the Bible gave the same advice that we should love others as we love ourselves. In other words, treat others how you would like to be treated.

If we approach others from a place of curiosity and respect, others will notice this, and they will be open and eager to communicate with us.

The other precursors to effective communication we spoke

about, namely being able to read social cues; and adapting behavior, language, and content to one's audience, are also critical when it comes to approaching new people.

People will receive us better if they are open to having a conversation with us in the first place, and if we speak in a 'language' they deem appropriate.

Poor Mike had to learn this the hard way:

Mike had a lot going for him, he was outgoing, friendly, and athletic, and he was used to having lots of women chasing after him. Given all of this, Mike had no issues with self-confidence and had no problem making conversation with anyone and everyone. However, that didn't mean that anyone and everyone wanted to have a conversation with Mike! One day, when Mike was training at the gym, as usual, he noticed a rather attractive young woman on the other side of the gym. She was on her own and had found a quiet corner of the gym to work out in. She had her headphones in her ears and seemed to be looking down at the ground a lot, avoiding eye contact with other members. Mike completely disregarded all of this, walked straight up to her, and tried to start a conversation. As he walked up to her, she completely turned her back on him, but Mike was too arrogant to notice this social cue, and he was determined to make contact anyway. I'm sure you can guess what happened next . . . the young woman angrily told Mike that the gym was not a place to 'pick up' women and that he should reserve his advances for women at the local pub. Mike learned a hard lesson in humility that day!

Fortunately (for us!), there are things we can do to prevent ourselves from falling into the same trap Mike and others have fallen into.

These 'things' relate to knowing how and whether to approach someone at all, as well as knowing what to say and what to talk about.

We are going to first tackle the challenge of how to know whether someone is open to having a conversation, as this is what you should be trying to establish before simply striking up a conversation with a random stranger.

How to Know Whether Someone Is Open to Having a Conversation with You

As we learned from Mike's situation, not *everyone* is open to having conversations *all* the time! It doesn't matter how friendly or confident you come across; not everyone is going to be just as friendly back to you.

So, what indicators should we look for before making the leap and starting a conversation with a stranger?

There are, in fact, three relatively reliable indicators we can use to help inform us about whether someone is open for a chat or wants to be left alone. These include paying attention to the SETTING you find yourself in; the CONTEXT; as well as SOCIAL CUES/BODY LANGUAGE from the other person.

To help you understand this better, we are going to go through each of these 'indicators' in more detail with some clear examples.

Why Setting Matters

The reasons why you'd go to a library, to a coffee shop, to a bar, or a business conference—I'm going to guess—are all quite different.

If you were to visit a library, it would likely be to find a good book to read or do some research, both of which are typically solitary activities done in silence. You probably wouldn't expect nor be impressed if someone tried to start up a conversation with you in the library, now, would you?

Compare this to your intentions when visiting a coffee shop. Perhaps you are lucky enough to have a break in your busy day and are looking to relax for a while, or maybe you're rushing to get to your next meeting, but you need a caffeine 'pick-me-up.' Or it could be that you're just tired of working from home, so you decide to take your laptop to your local coffee shop for a change of scenery. Whatever the case may be, a coffee shop certainly seems like the type of place where you'd be more open to having a conversation compared to the library. However, as we can see from these different examples, context would play a role, too, in how receptive you'd be to someone striking up a conversation with you. Context is something we will consider more in the next section.

Now, compare your reasons for going to the library or coffee shop to going to your local bar. What might your intentions be when visiting your local bar? Perhaps you'd be going out to catch up with some friends, or maybe you'd be on 'the prowl,' looking for other singles to connect with. A bar would probably be considered a much more 'open' and 'laid-back' setting to start a conversation with strangers. People tend to go to bars to enjoy themselves in the company of others, and alcohol can also make people more relaxed and open.

And we cannot forget about professional settings—think business conferences. What might people's intentions be in attending these types of events? Since these events are largely set up as networking opportunities, it would be safe to say this would be the type of setting where people would be very open to having conversations too.

Now that we have addressed the importance of the setting or environment you are in as an indicator of whether people may be open to having conversations, it's time to address context. Context is important because it gives us the 'bigger picture'—it tells us more than what a setting alone can tell us. In fact, we must assess 'context' together with the setting to determine whether it is appropriate to start a conversation or not.

1. What Is Context and Why Does It Matter?

Although the setting you find yourself in might help inform you about whether people may be more or less open to having conversations at all, as we saw when assessing the coffee shop setting, people can have different intentions for visiting the same place.

Recall that one of the strangers in the coffee shop was in a mad rush moving from one meeting to the next; another was preoccupied with doing their work, and another was taking time out to relax. Which one of these people do you think would have been open to having a conversation? Probably just the one that was taking time out to relax, we would guess.

How could we have known all of this about these different

coffee shop strangers?

The answer? Context.

To gauge whether someone would be up for a conversation with us based on context, there are a couple of things we can be on the lookout for. It helps to notice who the person is with: are they alone or with other people? If you're out at a bar and you're 'on the prowl,' and you see a table of ladies sitting together and there's a 'ladies' night' special going on that night, then those ladies are probably not out looking to get 'picked up.' They probably would not take your advances very well. Unless, of course, they had been staring at you and batting their eyelids all night . . . that boils down to reading body language cues and is something we will cover later too.

Another thing to look out for when it comes to assessing the context for clues on whether to approach someone is to notice whether the person looks preoccupied or distracted or whether they look comfortable and relaxed. For example, are they talking or texting on their phone or using their laptop? These are indications that they are probably not open to having a conversation and are likely tending to something important. It could also indicate that they don't want to be approached and are using their technological devices to indicate they are busy.

So, now, let's say you have acknowledged the setting and the context and feel that you have been given the 'green light' to go ahead and start a conversation. Well, there's still *one* more piece of the puzzle to solve before you jump in, and that is to assess the other person's body language.

2. Body Language That Indicates Openness to Conversation

Did you know that 70–93% of our communication is actually nonverbal? We are constantly sending out messages to other people without even realizing it. That's why assessing a person's nonverbal cues is such a powerful tool when it comes to discerning whether to approach them or not. Body language will tell you a LOT about what others are feeling and what they are thinking at any one time—it is an unspoken expression of what is happening internally.

Nonverbal communication or body language can include facial expressions, body movement and posture, gestures, eye contact, touch, space, and voice. When observing someone and deciding whether to approach them, we would just be concerned with those body language cues that are visible to us, which would be all of those mentioned except voice, touch, and gestures.

As we go through the body language signals that tell us whether someone is open to conversation or not, we will categorize them according to a traffic light system. If we talk about a 'green' light, we mean it is safe to approach when these behaviors are displayed, whereas if we talk about a 'yellow' light, it means to approach with caution, and if we talk about a 'red' light, it means it's best to avoid the person.

Nonverbal Communication Cues That Indicate Openness to Conversation

Cue #1: Facial Expression and Eye Contact

You can tell a lot about how friendly and approachable a person is by looking at their facial expression and whether or not they are avoiding eye contact with others.

Someone who is giving the 'green light' for conversation when it comes to their facial expression would likely have a neutral facial expression. Their face would essentially look 'relaxed,' or even 'expressionless.' There would be no raising or scrunching of the forehead, and their lips would either look like a straight line or be turned a bit upward in a slight smile. A person giving the 'green light' for conversation when it comes to eye contact would also likely be looking around at others and what is happening around them and would not appear to be completely avoiding eye contact with others.

Compare this to someone giving the 'red light' signal for conversation. This person's facial expression may come across as visibly upset, angry, or frustrated. You may notice them frowning, and their lips may be straight or turned downward, and their forehead scrunched up in a frown. They would likely be looking down, or at a phone or laptop, or just looking away from others in general—intentionally avoiding eye contact.

Note: Some people have a neutral facial expression that makes them appear upset, angry, or frustrated when they are not! If you haven't heard the term given to this in the popular media, it has been labeled 'resting bitch face,' which is kind of comical. Because 'resting bitch face' exists—that is people can appear 'mean' and 'unapproachable' just by their neutral facial expressions—it is important to consider all of their nonverbal cues, as well as setting and contextual cues together for the most accurate signal of whether to approach them or not.

Cue #2: Body Movement and Posture

A person's body movement and posture can also tell you a lot about whether they are open to being approached or not.

Green light signals from others include sitting or standing with their shoulders open and back and with their body turned toward others. Their hands, if visible, would usually be open versus clasped shut.

Red light signals when it comes to body movement and posture would include turning away from others, as well as having the arms folded and/or legs crossed. This kind of posture signals the person is closing him or herself off to others.

Note: Crossed arms can also indicate that someone is cold, and crossed legs can also just be a more comfortable way of sitting. So, these body language cues may be considered more as 'yellow' signals. This brings light to the fact that we need to consider someone's body language together with the greater context. Is it very cold, and is the other person rubbing their arms to keep warm? Are they crossing their legs but leaning back and smiling? These are things that need to be carefully considered.

Cue #3: Space

Another cue that can tell you whether someone is open to being approached or not is 'space.'

Let's say you're in a coffee shop and you notice that there are loads of free tables but that the person you're thinking of approaching has positioned him or herself at the table furthest away from everyone else. This is a pretty clear 'red' signal that this person probably doesn't want to be disturbed by others.

Compare this to somebody who sits in the center of the 'action,' even though there are many free tables further away from others. This person has not intentionally created space between him or herself and others, and so this can be considered a 'green' light.

Again, though, you need to consider the context: is the person sitting far away because they want to avoid others, or did they choose the 'far-away' table so that they could have a seat by the window with a view? And is the person sitting in the 'action' but intently focused on working on their laptop?

You see, this is why you need to assess the situation in its totality using the indicators at your disposal and make a judgment from there.

Now, we'd like you to put what we have taught you so far in this chapter into action. We have come up with an activity for you to try out to help you in your quest toward becoming a more effective communicator!

Activity 5: Observation and Approach

In this activity, you will work up to becoming confident enough to approach somebody you'd like to start a conversation with. To begin with, you will just be observing others and practicing the skills you learned earlier: looking for clues that people are open to being approached by examining the setting, context, and body language. This will help you build up the confidence to make your approach, which is ultimately what we will challenge you to do.

Step 1:

Think about some places you could go where you may find people who would be more open to having conversations with you. Think of places where people would be going to relax, for example, and where they would likely not be preoccupied or distracted and more likely be on their own. It will be less intimidating to approach someone who is on their own versus someone in a group.

Here are some examples of some settings and why they are good places to practice approaching people:

- A coffee shop. Coffee shops are great places for finding opportunities to practice approaching others. That's because people who go to coffee shops are usually there due to a break in their day or they have the time to be there and relax. So, they are more likely to be open to having a conversation.

- A bar. People who go to bars on their own often (but not always) do so because they are feeling lonely. Beware if you do approach them for a conversation, though. You might be in for a long one, especially if they have been feeling lonely and have had nobody to talk to for a long time!

- The mall. People who go to the mall are usually in a good mood—think retail therapy! A mall is a great place to approach people for a conversation because a lot is going on in the environment that you could use as a conversation starter. We will address how to use your surroundings to start a conversation in the next chapter.

- A park. The park is another great place to approach people because you will find lots of people in the park just relaxing and taking time out and who would likely be open to having a conversation. Like the mall, there is often lots going on at the park. You may see people exercising, walking or playing with their dogs, relaxing on benches, and more. Similar to the mall scenario, a lot is going on in the environment that you can use as a conversation starter.

- Public transport stops. When was the last time you had fun while waiting for the bus, train, or tram? Probably never. The same is true for others—people usually get bored waiting at public transport stops. There's not much you can do while waiting besides scrolling through your phone, maybe reading a book, or staring off into space! So what better place to approach someone for a conversation and make things less boring for you and them.

Step 2:

When you have identified somewhere to go, make your way there with a notepad and a pen. First, you are just going to 'people-watch.' Try to be inconspicuous about it—if someone notices you have been staring at them for hours, they may find it a bit creepy! Notice the indicators we spoke about and try to judge who may be more open to a conversation based on these.

Step 3:

If and when you feel confident and feel your judgment is fairly accurate—and you're getting a lot of 'green lights,' put your notebook away and try approaching someone. Keep the conversation light and short. You can just say hello and ask them how their day is going, for example.

Approaching Others

In this chapter, we have covered how to know when to approach others by paying attention to things in the external environment and by examining others' behavior.

In the next chapter, we are going to look more into what to do next now that you have mastered the initial approach. We are going to talk about how exactly to start a conversation and what to say.

Chapter 3 Key Takeaways:

- ✓ Knowing whether to approach others is 'easier' when we know what clues to look out for.

- ✓ We can gauge whether someone is open to having a conversation with us by examining the setting we find ourselves in, as well as the context and the other person's body language.

Chapter 4

The First Conversation – How to Open It and What to Say

"People appreciate when you speak their language."
— Sam Altman

It's one thing to know whether the opportunity is ripe to approach someone or not, but what is just as important is the words that come out of your mouth.

Women around the world can attest to this. Just think about the countless victims of all those incredibly famous yet cheesy pick-up lines. A popular one that comes to mind is, "Did it hurt? When you fell from heaven?" And we can't forget this one, "Do you believe in love at first sight? Or should I walk by again?" These pick-up lines and women's negative reactions to them prove that you don't need to craft what you think is a clever or interesting comment when starting a conversation with someone new. This can backfire because it can come across as disingenuous and manipulative.

It takes just 7 seconds to make a first impression, so if you get it right, you can expect to have a very positive interaction. Something that can help with this is to choose a conversation opener that is *appropriate* to your audience. Choosing an appropriate opener will help you make a good first impression, and a good first impression can make the difference between someone wanting to continue a conversation with you, or not.

In this chapter, we are going to go through some steps you can follow that will help you harness our 4th precursor of effective communication: adapting your behavior, language, and content to your audience. We will focus primarily on how to do this in the context of opening up the first conversation with someone.

Adapting Your Language and Content to Your Audience

How you speak to people and what you say to them depends on who the person is, in what context you are meeting them, and your 'goals' for the interaction.

For example, you would open up a conversation very differently with a colleague, a manager, a new potential client, a new potential friend, and a new potential mate.

We are going to look at a few different scenarios and provide you with the best way to tackle them by teaching you how to:

1. Clarify your intentions from the outset.

2. Assess your 'audience,' and

3. Assess the context.

Let's start by teaching you how to best start a conversation with people in your *professional* life.

When Your Audience Is People in Your Professional Life

We will use the example of going for a job interview and meeting a new potential client.

Before attending a job interview or meeting a new potential client, there are some steps you can take to help you know how to communicate in a way that will set you up for success.

Step 1: Clarifying Intentions

We need to know *what* we are hoping to get out of the interaction we're about to enter so that we know how to adapt accordingly.

For example, in the job interview scenario, the intention in going for the interview would be to land the job. So, to do this, we would be thinking about wanting to impress the interviewer so that we could stand out amongst the other candidates. Similarly, when meeting a new potential client, we would also probably want to make a good first impression. We would be looking to connect with and impress the client so that we could ultimately close the deal.

So, based on these goals, we know when opening up the conversation with the interviewer or client, we want to do it in a way that will impress them.

Step 2: Assessing the 'Audience'

Next, we want to ask the question, to WHOM exactly are we speaking?

In the example of the job interview and the new client meeting, we would have a much bigger advantage in knowing our audience than if we were meeting a random stranger.

In the case of the job interview and the client meeting, we would have specific information about the people we are speaking with ahead of time. For example, we would know such things as their name and their position in the company. Knowing this information would help us understand how to open the conversation because we would know how to address them.

For example, if you knew your interviewer's name was Melissa and that she was the HR Manager, you could greet her by her first name to open the conversation. When you introduce yourself, you could say, "You must be Melissa. I'm Michelle. It's a pleasure to meet you."

Step 3: Assessing the Context

In both of the examples—that is, the job interview and the new client meeting—the context is professional and business-like and therefore 'formal' to a certain degree. This means the way we greet our interviewer or new client needs to reflect this and be 'appropriate.'

You wouldn't walk into your potential new manager's office and high-five him or her! Instead, you would want to portray an image of 'professionalism' when introducing yourself by giving a firm handshake and making good eye contact. This doesn't mean you can't have some light-hearted conversation or you have to call the person by their formal title, like "Mrs. Harris."

Nor does it mean you have to refer to the person as "ma'am" or "sir," as you may have had to in school.

It just means you need to recognize that you are interacting with people who are probably going to be looking for and expecting professionalism in your behavior.

When Your Audience Is 'Random Strangers' in Casual Settings

Now, to address how to adapt your behavior, language, and content for casual settings, we are going to use the examples of having an initial conversation with a potential new friend and with a potential romantic interest.

Let's go through our steps again as they apply to these two scenarios:

First, we need to **'clarify our intentions.'**

What are we looking to 'gain' when approaching a potential new friend versus a potential romantic interest?

We would probably be looking to see if there is an initial 'connection' with the other person and perhaps, whether they would be open to hanging out in the future.

So given these intentions, how would we behave, what kind of language would we use, and how would we open the conversation?

We would probably be more 'casual' in our approach. We may not immediately introduce ourselves, but we may instead make a comment on something we notice about them as a conversation starter.

Let's look at an example of how you might start a conversation with a potential new friend first. Let's say you are walking down the street and you notice someone carrying a pair of ice skates, and you think this person could be a potential friend as you love ice skating and are in fact, an ice hockey player. So, you may use this 'common ground'—this mutual interest in ice-skating—to start a conversation with them. You might say something like, "Awesome skates—do you play ice hockey, too?" This could then lead to you talking about other topics and establishing whether you click with the other person or not. We will teach you more about small talk and keeping conversations going in Chapter 6.

Now let's look at how you might start a conversation with someone you're interested in romantically. Let's say you're at your local bar, and you notice an attractive man standing on the other side of the bar. Perhaps you notice he just ordered a shot of your favorite whisky—perfect conversation starter! You might say to him, "That's my favorite!" and to keep the conversation going, you might ask, "have you tried this other one?" or "have you always been big on whisky?" for example. Then, if the conversation has been going well and there is a connection, later on, you might drop a hint to gauge his interest level to decipher whether he may be interested in hanging out in the future. You might say something like: "Did you know that they do a whisky tasting at Jack's bar every Friday night?" If the other person responds excitedly and with enthusiasm, you could use this as a way to invite them to go to the next tasting with you!

The next step is to **"assess our audience."**

Casual settings, unlike business settings, do not allow us to 'know' our audience from the outset. We cannot, after seeing someone in a coffee shop, at a bar, at the beach, in a park, or on the street, go and look up their Facebook profile and get to 'know' them before approaching them. Even if we could do that, it would be kind of 'weird,' obsessive almost.

Compare this to doing 'research' on a company or client, which is very different and much more 'acceptable.'

So then, how can we get to *know* the stranger we want to approach without the advantage of having 'done our research?'

We can do this by using clues from the environment: how is the person dressed, for example, what coffee or drink did they order, and are they wearing any familiar labels?

These are all clues that can suggest what the person may be 'like' and how you can start a conversation with them. We don't want to encourage stereotyping people but noticing how people present themselves and how they behave certainly can say a lot about them—at least on a surface level.

Take, for instance, someone wearing an ACDC band t-shirt: this is a pretty obvious clue that they like the band and that they probably enjoy listening to other heavy metal music. It would be quite safe to approach this person by referring to their t-shirt and making a statement about the band if you were to be a fan too.

Now, what if the person you wanted to approach was a romantic interest? How might you 'assess' or get to 'know' them before approaching? Again, you would need to look for clues. For example, perhaps you both happen to be in an outdoor store, and you notice that they are about to purchase some high-quality hiking boots—what might this tell you about them? Probably that they like to hike! If you like to hike too, this would be the perfect opportunity to interject and tell them which boots you think are the best quality (if you have some knowledge of different brands!). This could then open up a conversation about hiking—you could go on to ask them, for example, where they plan on hiking next, and you can share your own love for hiking too.

The final step is to **assess the context.**

In situations where you would meet a potential new friend or potential new mate, the context would typically be quite casual.

There are no formalities, like in business meetings, for example, where you are expected to introduce yourself formally with a handshake and to give somewhat of a 'background' story.

In casual settings, when starting a conversation with someone new, you want to keep the conversation 'light' and 'friendly.' The number one tip for a conversation opener in this context would be to notice something about the person that you relate to or find intriguing. Noticing something that you relate to would look like our earlier example of making conversation with the ice skater because you're an ice hockey player or commenting on the ACDC t-shirt because you like the band too. These are examples of using the common ground to start a conversation. An example of noticing something intriguing may look like telling someone from your dance class that you really like their leggings and asking where they got them from.

From these initial conversation starter topics, the conversation usually takes on a life of its own. You could move on and talk about a number of things that 'flow' from the initial conversation about ice skating and leggings—you may go on to talk about what else they like to do in their spare time, what they do for work, and even where they may have traveled to.

So, now it's time to go out there and practice these skills in approaching new people—from clarifying your intentions to assessing your audience to assessing your context—you now have step-by-step instructions for how to adapt and change your behavior, language, and content depending on WHO you are speaking to.

Chapter 4 Key Takeaways:

✓ When meeting someone or starting a conversation with them for the first time, we need to be conscious of our behavior, our language as well as what we say.

✓ We can be informed about how to adapt our behavior, language, and content to our audience by clarifying our intentions, assessing our audience, and assessing the context.

Chapter 5

Your Actions Count Too

"Actions speak louder than words."
– Gershom Bulkeley (1692)

Isn't it incredible that this phrase is still used today, some 300+ years later? The message is still as true today as it was all those years ago. It doesn't matter what you try to say. If your actions don't align with your words, then the message you're trying to send will be totally misconstrued.

How we behave speaks volumes—we already learned that in the context of socializing and meeting new people—body-language counts for around 70–93% of how messages are sent and received between people.

In Chapter 3, we focused on the nonverbal messages that others send us and how we should receive them. Still, we have yet to examine the messages that we may be sending to others through *our own* body language and behaviors.

Being more aware of how we carry ourselves around others and sending open, friendly body language signals can not only help us make a good first impression, but it can also attract others toward us so that they feel comfortable approaching us too.

We can also use 'pro-social' behaviors as icebreakers when it comes to approaching new people. 'Pro-social' behaviors are behaviors we perform that are helpful to others, for example, holding the door open for somebody or picking up something somebody has dropped without realizing it and giving it back to them.

We are going to show you how you can use your body language to your advantage to indicate to others that you are open to interacting with them. Then, we are going to show you how you can use different pro-social behaviors to open up a conversation with others. Finally, we will teach you about mirroring and how you can use this body language 'trick' to build rapport.

In Chapter 3, we learned that we send body language signals to others through our facial expressions, body movements, posture, gestures, and eye contact. What you were asked to look for in others that indicated they were 'open' to being approached is what we are going to suggest you practice yourself, to come across as friendly and open too.

Let's return to what you learned about open body language, this time from the perspective of what YOU should be doing to let others know you are interested in them.

Using Body Language to Make an Impression

If you want to appear approachable to others, then you need to make them feel 'welcome.'

You can do this by making eye contact with others, and when they look back at you, flashing them a slight smile: this tells them you are friendly and interested in them.

If they smile back at you, then it's a great sign they are interested in you too. They might feel brave enough to approach you, but often, you'll have to take the initiative with the next move. This would look like 'ramping up' the nonverbal communication a level by either saying 'hello' or gesturing to them with a wave, for example. If they respond positively again, then you're all set for the approach. Before you walk up to them and start a conversation, though, you might want to take a quick glance over your shoulder. They may be smiling and waving at their friend who has just arrived to meet them, in which case you could end up with quite an awkward situation on your hands.

If you make eye contact with someone and they look away from you, or if you smile at someone and they frown at you or turn away from you, these are all signals they are probably not interested in having an interaction with you. Even if you come across as super friendly and approachable, there will always be people who just do not want to speak to you. So, it's best to use the feedback you get from the signals you send out to direct you on whether to approach someone or not.

When it comes to what to do with your body itself, you want to look relaxed. This means whether standing or sitting, your shoulders are down and back, and you are standing or sitting up straight. Your arms and legs should be uncrossed, and your hands should be open, not held in a fist. This kind of body language is what we would call 'open,' 'relaxed,' and 'confident,' and it indicates to others you are approachable.

Another important note is to be present and aware of your surroundings. This way, you will notice opportunities to connect with others. This also means putting away distractions like your mobile phone and laptop—anything that would signal you are preoccupied.

These are some simple yet powerful body language techniques

you can use to make sure you are sending others the right signals about your intentions to interact with them. They can also be used to gauge others' interest in interacting with you and help inform you of whether to approach or not.

Now, what about those pro-social behaviors we spoke about—those helping behaviors we can use to 'break the ice' and start conversations with new people?

Pro-Social Behaviors as Icebreakers for Conversation

As we mentioned already, pro-social behaviors are behaviors we perform that help others in some way or for the good of others.

Behaving in 'pro-social' ways, that is, noticing when others need help and offering it to them, can be a great conversation icebreaker. Wouldn't you recognize someone who tried to help you and who showed you kindness in a favorable way? We think so!

By being 'present' in the presence of others, you will become more aware of opportunities that arise to act in pro-social ways.

Here are some examples:

- Helping someone who has heavy luggage with them on the bus to get their luggage off the bus.

- Holding the door open for the person behind you.

- Offering to give someone money at the vending machine when you see they have realized they do not have enough money to get what they wanted.

- Offering your seat to an elderly or disabled person on public transport.

- Letting somebody with just one or two grocery items go before you in the line.

- Picking up something that somebody has dropped and giving it back to them.

No matter where you go or what you're doing, there are always opportunities to act in the best interests of others. When you help others out, you can use this as a conversation icebreaker. Take the first example of the person with the heavy luggage. You might ask them, as you're helping them take their luggage off the bus, where they are going to or where they have come from.

While pointing out that helping others is great in and of itself, and also great from the perspective that it's a great conversation starter, we do want to mention that you shouldn't 'abuse' it.

What do we mean by this?

We just mean you shouldn't go over and above to find ways to help or please others: if you're out and about and the opportunity arises, then sure, go for it! But do not make it your 'mission' to create opportunities where they don't exist. For example, let's say you see someone walking toward a door. Do not run ahead of them so that you can open it for them . . . that would make it very obvious what you're trying to do and would likely come off as quite manipulative.

It's also important to say that not everybody wants your help. Some people may reject your help, and when they are insistent, it's best to leave them to their own devices and walk away. You should always consider others' feedback when you approach them.

So, be kind when the situation warrants it; otherwise, keep using the other tips and suggestions we have provided so far.

Another body language trick we can use to help build rapport with people is called 'mirroring.'

Mirroring Others Builds Rapport

'Mirroring' refers to how we start to imitate others when forming a close relationship with them. We might mimic other people's tone of voice, their pace of speaking, the things they say, and their body language. The reason we mimic others is either to convey that we like them, that we trust them, or to show them empathy.

If you pay attention to other people interacting with one another, you will notice them mimicking one another, especially since the interaction they are having is positive. For example, you may see two people talking, and one of them puts their hand on their hip. Then after a minute or so, the other person does the same.

Or what about this . . . have you ever caught yourself using the same phrases, gestures, or behaviors as your friends or family? Maybe you never used to say 'ya know?' after every sentence, but since you started dating your boyfriend six months ago, you have taken on this quirk that used to really annoy you about him! This kind of mirroring tends to happen on a subconscious level between people who know one another well and who already have a close and trusting relationship.

So, if we know that mirroring occurs naturally and

subconsciously in people who like one another, then why not use 'mirroring' consciously as a way to build rapport with new people?

If you choose to use 'mirroring' to build rapport, the main thing to remember is that *subtlety* is the best policy. Have you ever played the 'copycat' game where you would copy everything your friend or sibling would do or say just to annoy them? . . . this is NOT what we are trying to do with mirroring.

So, what does mirroring look like then, and how can you practice it?

As we already discussed, mirroring looks like mimicking the person you're interacting with.

You can practice mirroring by starting small—try first to match the other person's tone and pace of voice. For example, if the person you're talking to is speaking quickly with excitement and enthusiasm in their voice, you want to respond in much the same way with the same level of excitement, curiosity, and interest in what they have to tell you. You will not build rapport by responding in a dull, flat, monotone voice. By the same token, you don't want to take imitating their voice as far as trying to copy their accent! That would just be odd.

If the person responds well to you mirroring their tone and pace of voice, you can try to mirror their gestures to some degree. For example, if they use their hands to make or emphasize a point, you can use your hands when speaking too. Make sure not to copy their every move, as it will come across as forced, and they may start to catch on to what you're doing.

You can also pay attention and mirror the other person's facial expressions. For example, let's say someone told you something really sad, like their dog died (as an extreme example!). They would probably have a very distressed expression on their face and may even start tearing up. You can match this by matching their expression—by also showing sadness and regret on your face. What you wouldn't want to do is try to force yourself to cry if they started crying. That would be taking things too far, and you should never have to force yourself to go to such lengths to mirror someone else. If it was a close friend you were talking with, now that might be different. You may be moved to cry without forcing it just because you are more emotionally invested in that person and probably would have known their dog, too!

So, if you decide to use mirroring to build rapport with new people, remember the basic rule: be subtle! If it feels too unnatural, then just don't do it.

Chapter 5 Key Takeaways:

✓ We need to consider the messages we send others through our own body language, as well as through our behaviors.

✓ We can create the impression that we are friendly and approachable by adjusting our body language.

✓ We can use 'pro-social' behaviors when opportunities present themselves as conversation icebreakers.

✓ We should always adapt our behavior according to others' positive or negative feedback.

✓ Mirroring is a great shortcut for building rapport with new people.

Chapter 6

What to Make 'Small Talk' About & How to Keep a Conversation Going

---

Small talk: you either love it or you hate it.

For many of us, the idea of making small talk can cause us to feel uncomfortable and awkward, and if you're an introvert, this kind of conversation can be altogether draining. But no matter how much we may hate it, small talk is a necessary starting point in any relationship.

Think about each of your nonfamilial relationships and how they started. We guess you didn't start talking about the meaning of life on the first day you met them (unless, of course, you happened to meet them in a Philosophy class!). The point is this:

building meaningful relationships take work, and we need to allow time for trust and connection to develop. This happens slowly through conversation on 'safe' topics that allow us to get to know someone better. We need to engage in small talk to get into deeper talk.

In Chapters 3 and 4, we spoke at length about how to know when others are open to conversation, as well as how to approach others and start a conversation. We did not really address what to do next, like how to keep the conversation going and what topics to talk about.

In this chapter, we are going to dive deeper into what to talk about with new people, whether in more casual settings or professional settings. We will also look at strategies for keeping the conversation going.

'Safe' Small Talk Topics

The advice to talk about certain topics and avoid others when it comes to meeting new people is nothing new. Most of us already know we should avoid topics like politics and religion around new people. We want to argue that although these topics should not be the first port of call, they don't have to be avoided like the plague if they do come up naturally in conversation.

For example, if somebody starts saying they believe in reincarnation and they feel their dog is actually their late grandfather reincarnated (again, extreme example!), it's okay to say what you believe if it is in opposition to that—as long as you state your view with respect and empathy. We will learn how to show empathy toward others in a later chapter. As a rule of thumb, though, we would suggest staying away from sensitive topics when conversing with new people unless they do come up naturally.

So, what topics *are* okay or better to talk about with new people, then?

The 'F.O.R.D' Strategy

This question has been asked so frequently that an acronym known as F.O.R.D. was created to help people remember what topics to talk about to help build rapport with new people. F.O.R.D. stands for family, occupation, recreation, and dreams. These topics are considered 'safe' because they are unlikely to lead to any stark differences in opinion, which can be touchy to navigate with people you don't know.

Question Lists Help but Not When They Disrupt the Natural Flow of a Conversation

It can be helpful to have a list of questions handy from each of these categories that you can draw from if you suddenly find yourself at a loss for words when in conversation with someone new. However, we want to make the point that it can be helpful to have some questions prepared on different topics, but it is always better if a conversation flows somewhat 'naturally' from one point or topic to the next.

For example, remember how, in Chapter 4, we spoke about how a great way to start a conversation with someone is by noticing something in the environment and using this as a conversation-opener? We gave the example of someone walking down the street with a pair of ice skates. We suggested that you could use the ice skates as a talking point if you were into ice skating too, for example, by asking the other person whether they play ice hockey. Does this sound familiar? Well, we want to go back to this conversation for a moment to demonstrate what we mean when we say that a conversation should flow somewhat 'naturally' from one point or one topic to another.

Example of a Conversation That Does Not Flow Naturally

Person 1: Awesome skates! I have a similar pair. Do you play ice hockey?

Person 2: Yes, I do, ever since I was 10 years old.

Person 1: Cool. Do you have any siblings?

This is what we want to avoid: changing the topic completely or blasting out questions just for the sake of having something to say. In an ideal situation, we would want to stick with the topic for some time and make a transition when it's warranted. Let's have a look at a better way to have approached this conversation:

Example of a Conversation That Does Flow Naturally

Person 1: Awesome skates! I have a similar pair. Do you play ice hockey?

Person 2: Yes, I do, ever since I was 10 years old.

Person 1: You must have picked up quite some skills then—are you playing professionally?

Person 2: Yes, I play for the Tigers, it's hard work, but it helps that my dad is the coach, and so he keeps an extra close eye on me.

Person 1: That's so cool. I wish someone in my family enjoyed skating as much as I do. Do you have any siblings?

You see, the family question fits much better here after there has been mention of a family member. There is a natural progression into a new topic that fits in the F.O.R.D. list of categories for safe conversation.

F.O.R.D. also tends to work well in instances where we have planned to meet up with someone we just met for a second time. For example, imagine you just met someone, and the initial conversation went really well—so well in fact that the person has agreed to meet up with you for a date. In second and later meetings, you would expect to be asking one another more questions because you are trying to get to know one another better. So, it makes more sense in this type of scenario to ask more of these kinds of questions.

It is important to note that, even though you may be talking about a 'safe' topic, you still need to be careful in how you ask your questions. Sometimes people have good intentions in asking a question but how they ask it makes their seemingly innocent question come across as rude and offensive.

Let's look at some examples to demonstrate what some good questions would look like compared to questions that may be a bit insensitive.

Good questions on the topic of family might look like:

1.) Do you have any siblings?

2.) Where do most of your family live?

3.) What does your father/mother/brother/sister do?

4.) Do you have a big family?

Compare this to asking the following questions, which are insensitive:

1.) When are you going to have children?

2.) When are you and your partner going to get married?

3.) Why are you still single?

The reason that these questions are insensitive is that they are presumptuous.

Asking people when they are going to do something assumes we know what other people are thinking or what they want for themselves. Imagine asking someone when they are going to have children, not realizing that perhaps they have struggled with fertility issues for years? And imagine asking someone when they are going to get married, not realizing that they are going through serious relationship problems or can't afford to get married. Asking 'why' questions is also not great as it comes off in an accusatory way. Asking someone WHY makes them feel judged. So before you ask a question, even if it is on a 'safe' topic, make sure you have considered how it might come across to the other person.

Activity: Coming Up with a Question List

Below we will provide you with a question list of five questions for each of the four F.O.R.D. categories (so 20 questions total) that you can use as a backup for future conversations. We would like you to add five additional questions of your own for each category. When you're done, go through the questions you wrote down and ask yourself about each one: am I judging or making an assumption here? If the answer is no, then your questions should be good to start using!

F – Family (since we already gave you four earlier, here they are again and one extra).

1.) Do you have any siblings?

2.) Where do most of your family live?

3.) What does your father/mother/brother/sister do?

4.) Do you have a big family?

5.) Where did you grow up?

O – Occupation

1.) What do you do for work?

2.) Do you like your job?

3.) What do you like most about your job?

4.) How did you get into <person's job>?

5.) What did you want to be when you were a child?

R – Recreation

1.) What are some of your hobbies?

2.) What sports do you enjoy?

3.) Do you consider yourself a creative person?

4.) If you had more free time, what would you do with it?

5.) What do you like to do at the weekends?

D – Dreams

1.) Do you have a bucket list of things you'd like to do in the future?

2.) If you could travel anywhere, where would you love to go?

3.) Could you see yourself living anywhere else in the world?

4.) Is there anything you would change about your life as it is right now?

5.) What is something you have always wanted to do but haven't yet?

Now get out a journal and see if you can add five more of your own questions to each category!

Where to Draw the Line – How Many Questions Is Too Many?

Another common piece of advice when it comes to keeping conversations going is to be curious and ask other people lots of questions. This is great, but we also don't want to turn a nice conversation into an interrogation. In an 'ideal' conversation, there is give and take on both sides: that is, both people should talk relatively equal amounts.

So, how can you strike this happy medium between being curious about the other person and asking them questions but also sharing about yourself?

Well, Dr. Carol Fleming came up with a great strategy to help us start and keep a conversation going. Dr. Fleming says that there are three components involved in starting and keeping a conversation and these include having an 'anchor,' 'revealing something,' and 'encouraging the other person.'

The first component, having an anchor, is something we already discussed in Chapter 3. This goes back to using something in the environment as a conversation icebreaker. For example, say you're in a hair salon waiting to see the hairdresser, and you want to strike up a conversation with someone who is also waiting. You could say something about the hair salon, like "Chi Chi's always has the best deals on hair!" Dr. Fleming calls these kinds of comments 'friendly noises'—they are not meaningful, but they are a polite and gradual way to enter into a conversation with someone else.

The second component is to reveal something about yourself that is related to the anchor you threw out. For example, you might continue your line of thought, saying, "I had been on the waiting list for weeks before getting this appointment today!" By sharing more information, you make the other person feel more comfortable sharing back and, at the same time, give them more information to respond to.

The third and final component is to encourage the other person to respond if they haven't already. The way to do this is by asking a question. For example, "Did you have a hard time getting an appointment too?"

As the conversation continues, you would stick with this formula: you respond to the person, share something about yourself, and then either wait for them to respond or ask a follow-up question.

The FORD approach is great for thinking about what to talk about in more casual settings, but what about when it comes to professional settings?

Let's have a look at what to talk about in these scenarios, which are both formal and professional.

What to Talk about in Formal, Professional Settings

When it comes to making small talk in scenarios that are more formal or professional, we need to be more strategic in our small talk. We can use what was taught in Chapter 4: to examine our goals for the interaction, our audience, and our context to direct us on what to make small talk about in these situations.

Let's use the same examples from Chapter 4—going for a job interview and having a new client meeting and think about what topics we could use for small talk in these cases.

Remember we mentioned in Chapter 4 that our goals for both interactions—the job interview and the new client meeting—would be to impress the other person and to stand out or close a deal. To do this, in the job interview, we would need to talk about our relevant skills and experience and what makes us a strong candidate above others. For the client meeting, we would need to talk about the client's problem, how our service or product offers a guaranteed solution, and how we are qualified to provide that solution. These are things we absolutely would have to cover: that we would be expected to cover.

Something to mention about the context of professional meetings is that they would probably have more of a 'structure' to them in terms of what you talk about and the order of what you talk about. For example, in the interview scenario, although the interviewer would be leading the conversation, the questions asked would likely flow from one to another and would be very focused on getting the information required (whether you're a great fit for the job or not!). Even your answers would be somewhat structured when it comes to explaining your relevant past experience.

In the case of meeting with a new client for the first time, there would be a way in which you would conduct this type of 'sales' meeting. It would probably start with you eliciting information about their problem, providing your solution, handling their objections, and finally, 'closing' the deal.

But what would we talk about at the beginning of the interview or meeting or toward the end? At these points, we would be able to use small talk to build rapport and improve the other person's impression of us to meet our goals.

One way we could impress the other person is by getting to know them, and we can do this ahead of time. If we do our research, we should find many things to talk about that would impress the other person. For example, we may find that the person we are talking to has been featured in the company blog or some other news article.

Imagine when it comes to the end of the interview, and the interviewer puts the ball in your court and asks if you have any questions, saying something like this: "I read about the project you were a part of in collaboration with Microsoft. It's my dream to be part of a project like that someday, and I'd love to know what the highlight of working on a project like that was for you." In doing this, you are making a personal connection— you are showing that you are genuinely interested in the other person while simultaneously showing that you are keeping up to date with important company news.

In the case of meeting a new potential client, it would be equally important to know some personal details about the client and the company they represent. This would be essential to know how to approach them to best address their problem and to have the best chance of 'closing' the deal. If you go into the business meeting having no idea how your product or service can solve your client's most pressing needs, then you may as well not have the meeting at all.

Okay, so now that you know what to talk about when making small talk and how to keep small talk going, it's time to do some troubleshooting as we move on to Chapter 7 and learn about what to do when a conversation goes wrong.

Chapter 6 Key Takeaways:

- ✓ When making small talk, it is best to stick to 'safe' topics.

- ✓ If sensitive topics come up, it's best to be empathetic.

- ✓ Keeping a conversation going requires a balance between sharing more about yourself and asking follow-up questions.

CHAPTER 7

What Happens When a Conversation Goes Wrong?

"One way to prevent [a] conversation from being boring is to say the wrong thing."

– Francis Joseph Sheed

Have you ever said the 'wrong thing' while speaking to someone? While sometimes saying the 'wrong' thing can make for an interesting conversation, it also has the potential to lead the conversation, as well as your relationship with the receiver to go south pretty quickly.

Take the example of Melissa and her friend Sharon:

Melissa had recently started going to Church, and she considered herself a 'new' believer—a 'new' Christian. She shared this information with her good friend Sharon, who was very spiritual, though not aligned with any one religion. Her religion was yoga, and she believed in such things as karma and the unlimited power of the universe working for the good of those who did good. When Melissa shared with Sharon that she had turned to Christianity, Sharon had a lot to say about that. Sharon started asking Melissa whether she thought that she would go to 'hell' as a nonbeliever, and she started to question Melissa on how she could believe in what was taught in the Bible, which she believed was extremely sexist toward women. Well, Melissa was stunned. She had only just started her Christian journey, and she was already being judged and bombarded with questions by her supposed 'good' friend. Sharon had, without realizing it, said all the wrong things, and Melissa was left feeling like she should never have shared her story with Sharon. In fact, she started to withdraw from her friend because she did not feel confident that Sharon would accept or respect her beliefs moving forward.

What happened here to make this conversation go so wrong?

Judgment and Lack of Empathy Lead Conversations to 'Go Wrong'

If we analyze how Sharon responded to Melissa's disclosure, we can see that Sharon judged Melissa and did not show much of that 'empathy' toward Melissa we spoke about earlier. Instead of hearing Melissa out and trying to understand why she had turned to Christianity, Sharon went straight in with her own assumptions and beliefs and started questioning Melissa's decision.

When conversations go 'wrong,' it is usually the result of a lack of empathy. This makes sense because if we are always striving to understand and respect the other person's perspective, how can there be room for rudeness or misunderstanding? Sure, we may still disagree with others and have our own opinions, but if we communicate our differences with respect and empathy for *others'* differences, then all of our conversations should go 'smoothly.'

This sounds all good and well, but the thing about conversations is this: there are two or more people involved. So, even if *we* have good intentions and show empathy toward *others*, we never know whether *they* will respond in the same way. We can only control our *own* part in the conversation.

So, to account for what happens when a conversation goes wrong, we are going to take a look at some different scenarios where this may happen and give you some tips for what to do in these cases.

First, let's look at some common scenarios in the context of meeting new people:

#Scenario 1: Meeting New People & Awkward Silences

There is a lot of room for error in conversation when meeting new people because there is a lot of guesswork involved. We do not know the person we are speaking to; we have only just met them! So we naturally have to be a bit more cautious about how we approach them and what we say, as we already learned in Chapter 3.

The following are some 'typical' ways that things can go wrong when conversing with someone for the first time and what to do about it:

What happens if you start talking to someone and there is an awkward silence? We already covered this in the previous chapter to some degree, but here the context is a little different. Here, we are covering what to do when you're talking to someone for the first time, and this happens.

We've all been there! Whether you dared to start up a conversation with a stranger or whether you're on a first date, awkward silences are an inevitable part of human interaction.

When you encounter an awkward silence, how do you start to feel, and what kind of thoughts do you have? A lot of the time, people start to feel uncomfortable and feel pressure to continue the conversation. They may even become super self-conscious and think the other person is judging them. This response, although normal, is not helpful.

There could be many reasons why the conversation fizzled out, and it is not always your fault! In fact, there's a good chance that the other person could be feeling just as you are.

So, take a deep breath, relax and allow yourself to feel the discomfort before making your next move.

Awkward silences usually happen when either you or the other person does not give sufficient information to continue the conversation, or for either side to continue asking follow-up questions, OR when the topic has been talked about at length, and there is not much more to say.

To avoid awkward silences in the first place, it's important to ask the other person open-ended questions and to answer the other person's questions 'fully.'

Open-ended questions are questions that allow the other person to give more than just a 'yes' or 'no' answer. For example, compare asking someone the question, "Do you like sports?" to "What kind of sports do you like?" In the first case, the other person can simply respond with yes or no, but in the second case, they are obliged to share more than just whether they like sports, and with more information, you have more to 'work with.'

Answering a question 'fully' means that when you are asked something, you do not just give a 'yes' or 'no,' or one-word answer. Say someone asked you a closed yes or no question—if you wanted to keep the conversation going, it would be best to answer yes or no but add some 'meat' to your answer. Say someone asked you, "Do you like to read?" Don't just answer, "Yes, I like to read." Tell them what you like to read! Tell them that you love crime fiction books, or that you love reading about personal growth and development, or if you hate reading, tell them what you like to do instead. This is what it means to 'fully' answer a question. Can you see that if you just said 'yes' or 'no' it may lead to silence because there would be nothing to follow up with . . . if you asked them the same question back and they also just answered yes or no, it would be the same predicament! You'd need to ask them for more details, for example, "Oh, you don't like books? What do you like to do in your free time then?"

Awkward silences can also happen when the other person is simply not interested in talking to you for whatever reason. A good way to identify this is if you start speaking to someone and they make an effort to only give you curt, closed answers and do not make any effort to ask you any questions back. You may also notice their body language as being closed—perhaps they have crossed their arms and are not making eye contact with you. In these cases, it is best to end the conversation. There is also a chance that the other person may be shy, but if that were the case, they would likely still make an effort, and it would be visible.

So, now that we have covered what may lead to awkward silences, what can you do when they happen?

Well, suppose the awkward silence is a result of not knowing what to say to continue the conversation, you can try to think about something you already spoke about that you may still be curious about—but perhaps the other person did not give you a full explanation. For example, maybe they told you they had worked abroad for a year before moving and settling where they are now. You could go back to this topic and ask them how their experience of working abroad was. People prefer to talk about their feelings, opinions, and experiences, so it's always good to ask them questions that prompt them to share these.

Sometimes the conversation might suddenly dry up—perhaps you have already talked about one topic at length, or the other person hasn't been very responsive. What can you do in this situation, and how can you change the subject?

Well, one way to do this could be to tune into your immediate surroundings and comment on something you can see. This will create a kind of 'distraction' and spark a completely new topic of conversation to talk about. For example, say you're at a restaurant having lunch: the conversation has died, and there's been silence for the past 2 minutes, which has felt like 2 hours! Look around at the decor in the restaurant and comment on something interesting, or comment on the music that is playing or anything else that you notice. For example, maybe the restaurant has many beautiful plants hanging from the ceiling. Noticing this, you might say something like: "Hey, what do you think about all those hanging plants? I've always wanted to decorate my apartment like that." See, just by simply noticing something in the environment and commenting on it—now a whole new and interesting conversation about home decor can begin!

If the awkward silence is the result of the conversation coming to a 'natural' end, where neither of you has much more to say, then you may want to think about simply ending the conversation. You can do this by stating that you enjoyed the interaction but need to go. For example, as you turn to leave, you could say something like, "Well, it was great chatting with you. It definitely made my Wednesday morning coffee break that much more interesting! Take care." If you'd like to see them again, consider whether it may be helpful to take down their number or exchange business cards.

Remember that lulls in a conversation or what seem like 'awkward silences' are pretty normal. Silences just feel more awkward when we are with new people because of the pressure we feel to keep the conversation going. But if you think about it, when we are hanging out with a close friend or family member, we often sit in long periods of silence together, and we don't think twice about it because the interaction is much more relaxed. We don't feel the same pressure to impress our friends or family as we do when interacting with someone new. Keep this in mind the next time you experience an awkward silence.

#Scenario 2: Meeting New People & Brashness

Sometimes it happens that, even if we identified every green light indicating that it was 'safe' to approach someone, when we actually do approach them and start talking to them, we find out that we read the signals 'wrong.'

Have you ever been in a situation where you noticed an attractive person smile and wave at you? You may have felt flattered and waved back only for their partner to come running right past you into their arms, just about knocking you off your feet in the process. This is an example of reading the signals wrong. Usually, when we get our wires crossed, the signals we are trying to interpret are much more subtle than a wave, so it can be easy to get our wires crossed.

So, what can we do when we have worked up the courage to approach someone only to be shut down by them?

If the person you have approached starts to act rudely toward you immediately, there are two ways in which you can handle this.

The first way is applicable when, for example, the person has assumed your intentions. You can first try to clarify your intentions and see if they soften. If they do, then you can go ahead and continue the conversation. Let's say you tried to start a conversation with an attractive person by offering to buy them a drink at a bar. They may have been giving you all the signs that they were open to an approach, but for whatever reason, when you made your move, they were unimpressed. Let's say they told you, "I can buy my own drinks." How do you bounce back from a comment like this? The way to do so is to humble yourself, apologize, and state your intention, then try to continue the conversation. For example, you could say, "I apologize if my offer offended you, I was hoping to have a chat, and I noticed you were here alone too. My name is Michael (hold out your hand to introduce yourself to the other person)." If the other person responds favorably after you have apologized and stated your intentions, then you can take that as a sign to continue the conversation. However, if the other person is still reluctant or continues being rude toward you, it is best to walk away. As we said already, not everyone wants to talk to anyone and everyone all the time, and you shouldn't force anyone to talk to you.

What about if a person you approach gets very angry and starts yelling at you? We seriously doubt that this would happen, but you never know. In this case, the solution is simple—walk away. This person, if they are already so upset, is probably not going to suddenly switch and become cool, calm, and collected. There is probably something else going on with this person, as most people would not act in such an aggressive manner even if they were not interested in speaking with you. We never know what might be going on in somebody else's world: maybe they just lost their job, maybe they just found out their partner cheated on them! We just don't know, and that's why we should always choose to be kind, and part of being kind and empathetic is knowing when to walk away from a situation.

#Scenario 3: When the Conversation Becomes a Heated Debate

When going into a conversation, we often intend that it will be casual and friendly. But sometimes, before we know it, we find ourselves in the throes of a heated debate!

This can happen whether we have met someone new or whether we are having a conversation with a close friend or family member. As we mentioned already, the reason why this tends to happen is because of a lack of 'empathy'—that is, a lack of understanding, acceptance, and tolerance for another person's view. We can debate healthily, but when others start to judge, criticize, belittle and use other means to disrespect our views, that is when we know that the conversation has taken a turn for the worse and is headed down a slippery slope.

There are a few topics that most communication books will tell you to steer clear of, especially when conversing with people you just met: for example, politics and religion are often cited as big 'no-no's' and as topics to be avoided at all costs when speaking to new people. The reason for this is that these topics are topics that people take very seriously, and that people are often divided on.

Imagine this: someone you just met starts preaching to you about all of the problems in government. They tell you about how Trump was the best president ever and how America will never be great again. Let's say you hold a different, almost polar-opposite view, and try to share this (respectfully) with this person. Remember how we said earlier that we can control how we speak to others and what we say but that we can't control how they speak to us and what they say? Well, many times, and especially if the other person doesn't really know you and the two of you have not built up much rapport, that other person may become easily offended or defensive. Even if you are being empathetic in your approach, you may still get some backlash from them.

So what are your options in this case?

You could either decide that the conversation is not worth having and end it. You could tell the person, "I really do not feel that this conversation is going anywhere, and I have to get back to work," and then physically remove yourself from the conversation.

Or, if you would like to keep the conversation going but would like to tone things down, you could try to put the fire out. In this case, you could tell them, "While I respect your opinion, it seems like you are unwilling to hear or understand mine. I am willing to continue this conversation if you are willing to respect that my opinions are different from yours." If the person is rude back to you or gets even more defensive, then you may want to consider ending the conversation here. However, if they acknowledge that they have been acting unfairly and can see eye to eye with you, then it should be fine to continue. You could also suggest changing the topic, for example, "It seems we have some very different opinions on this topic. I'm not sure that this conversation is leading anywhere productive. Why don't you tell me more about . . ." In both cases, even though the conversation has become quite heated, you can create an opportunity to redeem it and positively interact with the other person.

You can use these same strategies whether conversing with a stranger or with a close friend or family member. If somebody is not showing you respect, you have the right to walk away and refuse to communicate with them.

Now let's look at some common work-related scenarios in which conversations may go wrong and what you can do about it.

#Scenario 4: When Things Get Weird at Work

We can think of many work-related situations where conversations may become strained. For example, having a disagreement with a colleague or manager, being reprimanded, sharing ideas, asking for a salary increase, and more.

Work situations are a bit different, and there is more of an incentive to keep our professional relationships intact since we have to see the people we work with every day. We can't just 'walk away' from a conversation with someone at work as easily as we can with a stranger, friend, or family member.

So, let's look at different work conversations and discover what to do when they 'go wrong.'

Have you ever tried to share your ideas in a work meeting, but you keep getting shut down as soon as you utter so much as a sound? We bet that it doesn't make you feel like a very valued employee. It probably also leaves you wondering how to address such a problem. How do you go about speaking to the person who is never prepared to listen? Well, the best thing to do would be to go and have a one-on-one conversation with the person. It is better to settle this one-on-one because it will show the other person that you are serious about having your voice heard, and they will also be less likely to get defensive than if you raised your concern in front of others.

The 'agenda' for this kind of conversation would be to 1.) state your intention, 2.) state the facts, 3.) state how you felt, 4.) hear their side, and 5.) come up with a mutually agreed-upon solution. We will go into this in more detail later when we talk about constructive conflict resolution, but here is an example of how this conversation might go:

What Happens When a Conversation Goes Wrong?

1. Provide your intention – before starting a serious conversation with someone, it is important to inform them of what you'd like to discuss so that they do not feel caught 'off-guard.' If they know beforehand what will be discussed, they can be prepared and know what to expect.

You might state your intention in the following way: "I'd like to have a conversation with you about how we interact in our meetings. Do you have some time to chat this afternoon?"

2. State the facts – it is important when making your 'case' to stick with the facts and not to blame the other person for how you are feeling. It's recommended to say how you feel but to own your feelings.

Here is an example: "When I have tried to share my ideas in meetings, you tend to cut me off before I have had the chance to make my point (the facts). It makes me feel that my ideas are not valued (sharing but owning your feelings).

3. Hear their side – it's important to let the other person speak and explain their side and for you to show understanding whether you agree with their logic or not.

For example, maybe they tell you that they do want to hear your ideas but that they need to manage the meeting time. Let them know that you hear what they're saying and that you understand.

4. Come up with a mutually agreed-upon solution – once you have both been able to share your sides, you need to figure out how to solve the problem together. This is the part where you can start to make suggestions.

For example, "Okay, I hear what you're saying about time being an issue. I wonder how we can move past this. I wonder how we can keep our meetings to 60 minutes but also make sure there is time to share ideas. How about if we dedicated 10 minutes at the end of each meeting for people to share their input?"

You could use this same strategy if you have disagreed with a colleague or manager. It is important when you have a conflict to address it early and to find ways to move forward positively and productively together. Remember, when it comes to business, 'teamwork makes the dream work.'

#Scenario 5: The Dreaded Salary Conversation

Here's a conversation we all need to have at some point but all dread: asking our employers for more money. Asking for a salary increase is a sensitive topic, and it needs to be approached in the same way.

The conversation can go horribly wrong if your employer thinks that you are being unreasonable. You don't want to come across as ungrateful, but you know your worth and that this salary increase is warranted. It may not be a case of just wanting more because you are more experienced now or have started taking on more responsibility. There are other factors to consider, too, like inflation and the rising cost of living.

Whatever the case may be, you have the right to ask for a salary increase, so what is the best way to do it to avoid the conversation going 'wrong?'

Well, timing is important as a first consideration—most salary reviews happen on an annual basis but not all companies will suggest having a formal review. So, if your contract states you should have an annual salary review, and it is coming up to a year you have been with your company, and they have not mentioned the annual review, then you need to take the initiative.

Stating the facts is particularly important when asking for a salary increase because you are working with figures, which can be quite a sensitive topic. To keep things strictly business and strengthen your case, you can actually back up your new ask with data. For example, you could present to your boss that you had been making X amount last year and the same amount this year so far, but inflation has increased by X amount, and your salary has not increased with inflation. You could even present a salary survey, including data about how much someone with your job title should be earning, with your experience and qualifications. Make sure that whatever you propose is fair and backed up with evidence, and you won't go wrong. Once you have presented the facts, make sure to give your boss some time to review your proposal and get back to you.

Now, let's look at what to do when the conversation doesn't go as planned in CLOSE relationships.

Conversations can go just as wrong when we communicate with people we care about as they can with people we don't know so well. In close relationships, the ability to manage conversations that go wrong is even more crucial because we are already invested in these relationships. So when they go wrong, they tend to have more of an impact on us when things are left unsaid or issues are left unresolved.

The reason for conversations going wrong when we communicate with people we are close to is just the same as what goes wrong in all other miscommunications. Misunderstandings and disagreements can always be traced back to judgment and a lack of empathy creeping into the conversation.

You're probably familiar with the classic portrayal of the ignorant and insensitive husband. His wife asks him, "Honey, do these jeans make my butt look big?" And he answers, "You mean bigger than usual?"

And what about the scene that plays out in just about every other horror movie. You know, the one where the couple set off on this amazing adventure and wind up getting lost. What started out as a blissful Sunday drive quickly turns into a screaming match when the couple starts to panic, and each blames the other. The partner who has been driving insists if THEY had been the one reading the map, then they wouldn't have been lost, and the other insists they should have stopped ages ago and asked for directions.

Close relationships can quickly turn sour and start to break down if a conflict is not resolved effectively. There are healthy and unhealthy ways of approaching conflict. Some people avoid conflict altogether—they would rather not deal with the discomfort of raising an issue, and they may fear the other person's reaction. This is not healthy as it builds resentment and creates distance in relationships. Others compete, as we saw in the example above, where the couple started blaming one another because each wanted to be right and 'win' the argument. Others overaccommodate when it comes to conflict resolution, meaning they take on all the blame and try to fix things. This is unhealthy because this behavior, like conflict avoidance, also leads to resentment. The healthy way to solve a conflict, then, is through compromise. To compromise, both people need to hear one another out and come to a mutually workable and acceptable solution.

So, how do you solve a conflict healthily and become an expert compromiser?

The next time you're having a conversation with a close friend, partner, or family member and they say something to upset you, or you have said something to upset THEM, follow the steps we are going to detail below:

Step 1: Recognize What Caused the Problem

So, someone close to you has said something that has caused you to feel hurt. What was it about what they said that hurt you?

For example, maybe you were eating a snack before dinner time, and your partner said to you, "Are you really going to eat that before dinner?" Let's say this comment made you feel upset because you felt your partner was judging your eating habits.

When you have understood why what the other person said has caused you to become upset, it's time to look at the situation from their perspective. Think about why they may have said what they said? Perhaps they were preparing a nice dinner and felt that you eating a snack beforehand would ruin your appetite for the meal.

The point in asking yourself these questions is to understand the problem from both your own and the other person's perspective.

Step 2: Communicate the Issue

When you have examined both sides and come up with a relatively objective view of the scenario, it is time to make yourself feel heard and confront the issue.

There is a skillful way to do this so that the other person does not go on the defensive and start a full-on argument or debate. It involves stating the facts and owning your feelings.

What does this look like?

Well, using the example above, you might say the following to your partner:

"I wanted to talk about your earlier comment about me eating a snack before dinner. When you asked if I was really going to eat what I was eating, I felt judged, like I had done something wrong."

Compare this to: "You really made me feel like shit earlier when you made that comment on my eating habits. I don't know why you have to be so rude sometimes."

As you can see, when you state the facts of the situation in a straightforward way and take ownership of your feelings without blaming the other person, it sends a very different message.

If YOU are the one who has hurt someone else, we are going to look at how to apologize when we go through the next step, step 3.

Step 3: Apologize, Forgive & Compromise

The next and final step is to apologize if you are the one who is in the wrong, to forgive if you are the one who has been hurt, and then come to a compromise.

If the conversation has gone wrong because of something you did or said, then you should make a heartfelt apology before trying to come up with any solutions or compromise. A genuine apology includes a statement of what you are sorry about, consideration for how your words may have made the other person feel, and a commitment to how you plan to avoid hurting the other person's feelings again in the future.

So, let's say that you were the one who commented on your partner having a snack before dinner-time.

A genuine apology would look like this:

"I am sorry for criticizing your eating habits. I can see how doing so made you feel judged. I should have told you I was concerned that the snack would ruin your appetite for the nice meal I had prepared. I will say how I feel in the future instead of making critical comments."

Notice how in this apology, there are no conditions, there are no buts, no sarcasm, or anything that would undermine the apology.

Compare that apology to the following one:

"Sorry for criticizing your eating habits, but I just think that eating a snack before dinner ruins the meal."

How would this apology make you feel? Probably not much better. So make sure when you apologize, you do so genuinely.

If you are the one that needs to forgive, then you should do so quickly and with an open heart: holding a grudge will not help move things forward.

Finally, Compromise!

The final part of resolving conflict, and the most important, is to come up with a compromise—a solution that both parties contribute to and both parties are reasonably happy with.

Sometimes it makes sense for both sides to change their future behavior, but in the example above, it wouldn't really make sense for you to stop eating a snack before dinner just because your partner believes it will ruin your appetite for the meal. It would be different if, for example, you always tended to have a big snack before a meal and then never finished your meals. So, the compromise should be fair and make sense in the context of the conflict.

So far in this book, we have covered effective communication mostly from the perspective of meeting new people. In the final chapter, we are going to look at the role of effective communication in more intimate relationships.

We will look at how to build closer relationships in two ways: how we talk to others and what we talk about.

Chapter 7 Key Takeaways:

- ✓ Sometimes conversations go wrong, even when we have the best intentions.

- ✓ Conversations go wrong when there is judgment and a lack of empathy.

- ✓ We can steer conversations back on a good path if we know how to respond/act.

- ✓ But we also need to know when to leave/end a conversation that is going nowhere.

Chapter 8

Taking Conversations to the Next Level & Moving Relationships From Superficial to Meaningful

"Communication to a relationship is like oxygen, without it, it dies."

— Unknown

It's all good and well to be able to approach new people and make new connections—but having this skill on its own? Not so useful. As the quote suggests, without ongoing and effective communication, there is no relationship.

We're quite sure you didn't purchase this book just so that you could learn how to talk to people for the fun of it. I mean, sure, it can be nice just to strike up a conversation for fun, and not every conversation has to have a goal attached to it. Take the story of Matt, for example:

Matt was traveling from university to visit his long-distance girlfriend for the weekend. At the train station, while waiting to leave, Matt's train was delayed. So, while he was waiting, he decided to grab something to eat at Burger King. He noticed a middle-aged woman sitting on her own and looking lonely, so he decided to ask if he could join her. The two of them had a great conversation, and it turned out that she was working in the HR department of a company where he had applied for an internship! We're sure you can guess what happened next . . . this casual conversation that was without a goal actually ended up with Matt getting the internship he was hoping for!

So, sometimes having a conversation with someone just for the sake of it can lead to some surprising and unexpected outcomes. However, more often than not, when we are thinking about talking to others, we do have a goal in mind.

So what kind of goals do people usually have in wanting to learn how to be better communicators? Some that come to mind and we have already touched on include making new friends, finding a life partner, and building a business network. We have already learned about how to do these kinds of things, but we haven't learned about what to do next.

Say that you've managed to make a new acquaintance or to find someone who wants to see you for that second or third date. What communication skills are needed from this point onwards? How do you take that new acquaintance, for example, and develop a meaningful friendship with them? You see, there's no point in making new connections if you're not sure how to sustain them.

When it comes to building closer connections with other people, two of our effective communication precursors come to mind: 'showing genuine interest and concern for others' and 'adapting behavior, content, and language to your audience.'

Showing genuine interest and concern for others is another way of saying we need to show empathy toward others. Empathy is what creates trust and safety in a relationship. When there is trust and safety in a relationship, people feel more comfortable being vulnerable and opening up. If adequate empathy is shown, then people 'adapt their content' accordingly—they move from talking about safe, small talk-type topics to much deeper ones.

So moving a relationship from a superficial level to a deeper one involves communicating in an empathetic style, together with mutual self-disclosure or mutual sharing on topics beyond just small talk.

In the next part of this chapter, we are going to take you through what it looks like to demonstrate empathy toward others, as well as provide some steps on how you can start to practice empathetic communication right away. Then, we will teach you more about self-disclosure and how to move your conversations gradually past the small talk to build closer relationships.

What Empathetic Communication Looks Like & How to Practice It

"Empathy is the capacity to think and feel oneself into the inner life of another person."

– Heinz Kohut

In Chapter 7, we learned that when conversations 'go wrong,' it is usually because of a lack of empathy on one or both sides, together with judgment.

If you are interested in building positive relationships with the people you talk to and deepening these relationships, then demonstrating empathy toward others is vital. Empathy allows us to cut through the superficial so that we can develop more meaningful connections with others. When we act with empathy toward others, it makes them want to open up and share more with us because it feels safe to do so.

In conversations with others that are marked by empathy, we tend to leave such conversations feeling good afterward and really connected to the other person.

When there is a lack of empathy from the other person, the conversation tends to look and feel something like this:

- It felt like they just weren't listening to you. They may have been nodding their head and agreeing with you, but it felt as though their mind was elsewhere.

- They kept interrupting you, or they couldn't wait to share their own point of view without really letting you finish what you were saying.

- It felt like they didn't truly understand what you were saying. They were very quick to provide a solution or dish out advice.

If any of these scenarios is familiar to you, then you know what it feels like when the person you are speaking to is not really hearing or understanding you.

When we don't feel seen, heard, and understood by others, it makes us feel that what we have to say is not valuable. It puts us in a position where we do not feel comfortable sharing with this person in the future because we think: what is the point if they don't really care or listen to us anyway?

This is why the quality of being 'empathetic,' represented by our 'precursor 2' to effective communication, 'showing genuine interest and caring for others,' is crucial when it comes to speaking to people. No matter who it is, all people crave to feel understood, heard, and accepted by others, and as we learned in Chapter 2, being empathetic increases likeability.

If we can be empathetic in our interactions with others, we will build trust—the essential building block of all relationships.

So, with this in mind, we are going to reveal to you what it TRULY means to be empathetic and also teach you how to cultivate empathy in your conversations with others.

But First: What Does It Mean to Be Empathetic?

One way to understand empathy is to compare it to sympathy.

Sympathy is when a colleague tells you they are feeling sick and won't be coming to work, and you feel 'sorry' for them. You may think of a time when you also felt sick and did not go to work. You may feel sympathy for them because you know what it was like for yourself when you were in that situation: it made you anxious about having to catch up on lots of work when you eventually went back to the office. In this scenario, you feel 'bad' about your colleague's situation because you can relate to it from your own experience.

Compare this to empathy: empathy is when you do not make assumptions about the other person's experience based on your own experiences. When you show someone empathy, you are not just telling them that you feel 'sorry' for them or that 'you know' how they feel. Empathy goes much further than this: empathy tries to understand the other person's experience from *their* perspective.

For example, say your friend tells you that they are really struggling to concentrate on the material they have to study for an upcoming exam. If you wanted to show empathy, you wouldn't assume they were struggling for the same reasons you perhaps struggled to study in the past—let's say, for you—it was a lack of sleep. Instead, you would make an effort to ask questions that would allow you to know and appreciate your friend's unique experience: what exactly is making it hard for them to concentrate, and how is that affecting them?

Do you notice the discrepancy here between sympathy and empathy?

Another key component of empathy is that when you empathize with someone, you 'validate' their experience.

Let's look at an example of a conversation to demonstrate this:

Perhaps you are having an argument with your partner over whose turn it is to do the dishes. After a heated debate, you finally say to them:

"I work all day long and look after the children. The least you can do is help out with the dishes every now and then."

A response that lacks empathy (from your partner) would look something like this:

"Fine, I'll do the dishes this time, but you can take out the trash next time."

This response shows no concern for how the other person is feeling or why they are feeling the way they are feeling.

Compare this to the following very empathetic response:

"It sounds like you're feeling unappreciated. I haven't given you much recognition lately for the sacrifices you make for our family on a daily basis."

Can you see how, in this second example, the partner has made an effort to try to understand *how* his wife is feeling and *why* she may be feeling how she feels?

How much better would you feel if *you* were in this situation and your partner treated *you* with empathy?

Hopefully, these examples drive the message home about the importance of empathy in building positive relationships with others.

We can practice empathy with others whether we have just met them or know them on a deeper level, as in the example above. All that is needed to show empathy, in either case, is an adjustment in the way we listen to and respond to people.

In counseling, practicing empathy is a skill that counselors have to master to build open and trusting relationships with their clients.

Borrowing from the counseling practice named after famous, person-centered therapist Carl Rogers, we are going to teach you how you can practice this important skill through 'attentive listening.'

What Is Attentive Listening and How Can We Practice It?

What attentive listening is, is implied by the word 'attentive'—

we can think of attentive listening as being present when we listen to others.

It doesn't sound too difficult, right?

Yet many of us, if we have to admit it, are not the best listeners and find ourselves on the other end of those 'scenarios' we mentioned at the beginning of this chapter. In conversations, we get distracted, become more focused on what we would like to share next or give unsolicited advice. More often than not, in one way or another, we don't give others the attention they deserve.

By practicing attentive listening, we can break our bad habits and give people the opportunity they long for—to share and to feel heard—which will grow and strengthen our connections with them.

Below, we are going to provide an example of a conversation between two people who just met, and we are going to show you how to practice 'attentive listening' in this context:

Person 1: So what brought you to Michigan?

Person 2: Well, it's kind of a long story, but I moved here to complete my Ph.D. in Sociology.

Person 1: Wow, that is a long way to move for your studies, especially since you mentioned that you really loved living in Australia.

Person 2: Yes, it is. You see, the thing is, I never really had much of an option. The programs in Australia had very competitive entry requirements, and I had already gone through the process twice . . . it was grueling, to say the least! And I just couldn't stand to go through it again. So when I saw the program here and I checked out the application process, I was quite relieved as it seemed to be much smoother. And as it turns out, it was!

Now we are going to show you how you can respond to this comment using strategies that promote 'attentive' listening and, therefore, empathy.

1. It's all about the feelings

As we already learned, empathy is about being able to understand things from the other person's perspective, and what better way to do so than to identify how they must be/must have been feeling.

In the last comment from Person 2, we learn about how their university application process was 'grueling' and how they just couldn't 'stand' to go through it again. We also learned that now, having been through it and having found a solution, they feel 'relieved.'

The feelings we can identify are initial pain and disappointment followed by calm and ease.

So, now that we have identified how we think the person must have felt and feels now, how can we communicate our 'understanding' of the situation to them so they feel heard and understood?

2. Summarize

In our own words, we can communicate our understanding of what the person has just told us by summarizing the 'gist' of the situation and how they must have felt and currently feel.

For example:

"Wow! It sounds like you experienced a lot of disappointment before finally getting accepted into your Ph.D. program, but it seems like you're quite happy with the way things worked out in the end?"

In this response, we have mentioned how the other person must have felt in the past (disappointed) and now (happy/satisfied) while also summarizing the contents of what they told us.

This response shows that we have really listened to and are trying to understand what was said. This signals to the other person that we genuinely care about what they have to say.

3. Clarification

'Clarification' is the final part of active listening, and it often looks like asking someone a question to test your assumptions or understanding of what they have said.

In the example above, we are seeking clarification by stating that 'it seems like you're quite happy?'

We do not know for sure when the other person said they were 'relieved' if this meant they were happy. For example, the person may have felt relieved that they got into the program, but they could be hating the fact that they were now living in a strange new town as a result. Or, they could be relieved and really happy with how things worked out—maybe they were thrilled, and having to move to the new town was better than they had expected. We wouldn't know unless we asked for clarification.

We can also ask for clarification by asking more straightforward questions, such as, "What do you mean by that?" or "I'm not sure I understand," or, "Would I be correct in saying that . . .?"

The main rule of thumb when it comes to asking people questions for clarity is to avoid asking WHY at all costs. The reason being is that 'why' questions often come across as accusatory—to give you an idea, imagine you're on your fifth date with someone, and the topic of past relationships comes up. Now, imagine your date tells you about how their previous partner dumped them, and you'd like to know more . . . which way of asking for clarification sounds better?

1. *Why* did he dump you?

2. *What* do you think was the main reason for the relationship breaking down?

We're going to assume that you picked Number 2.

Can you see how 'why' questions tend to make assumptions: "Why did he dump you?" sounds like we are on the ex-partner's side, and we want to know what is wrong with our date. Whereas in Number 2, there are no assumptions. The 'what' question comes across as more neutral and asks for the person's OWN perspective on the situation.

Now that you have understood the significance of being

empathetic in your actions with others, we would like to challenge you to go out and practice your attentive listening skills. You can start by practicing with your close friends and family members—see if they notice any difference in your communication style and whether they open up more to you!

Next, we want to teach you how to deepen your relationships through what you say and share with others—otherwise known as 'self-disclosure.'

What Is Mutual Self-Disclosure & How to Use It to Move Conversations to the Next Level

If you want to move a relationship to the next level, you need to be willing to share your authentic self with others. We learned about why it is important to be authentic in Chapter 3. We learned that people like people who are 'real' and true to themselves.

You cannot get close to others and wear a mask at the same time. Many people can't shake the fear of rejection when it comes to sharing about themselves with others, and some are just not used to nor comfortable with the spotlight being on them. But at some point, you need to take the mask off: you need to take the risk and allow yourself to be vulnerable if you want to connect with people beyond the small talk.

So what exactly does mutual self-disclosure look like, and how do you practice disclosing things about yourself to others?

Mutual self-disclosure is the mutual sharing of information about one another that occurs between two people in conversation with one another. In an ideal conversation, two people talk and share things about themselves relatively equally. At the beginning of a relationship, sharing is reserved for shallow topics, like the safe topics for small talk we spoke about in an earlier chapter. People tend to share cautiously at first, but as the relationship develops and trust builds up through repeated sharing and repeated favorable responses from the other person, people begin to share more personal information. This is how close relationships develop.

But how do you go from talking about your favorite meals, how many dogs you have, and how you love football to talking about your spiritual beliefs, your plans for the future, and your greatest fears?

Well, the key is to start small and gradually move things forward depending on the type of feedback you get from the other person. You should start to find that the more you share with others, the more they will likely share with you too. If the other person responds to what you share with empathy and kindness, this is a positive sign too.

We like to think of there being about 4 'levels' of self-disclosure, where level 1 represents the least risky things to share with others and 4, the riskiest. When we talk about something being more 'risky' to share, we just mean that it is riskier from an emotional perspective because the more personal details you share about yourself, the more you open yourself up to judgment or rejection. That's why it is important to share more personal details as the relationship develops more trust.

Let's take a closer look at the 4 'levels' of self-disclosure that we propose exist.

Level 1: Sharing facts about yourself with others: this would include things like your name, where you are, whether you have a pet, how many siblings you have, what you do for work, and what you do for fun.

Level 2: Sharing your opinions and beliefs: this would look like sharing your religious background, sharing your political views, and sharing what you think about some or other current affairs.

Level 3: Sharing your hopes and dreams, for example, whether you'd like to have children, where you'd like to live, and your career aspirations.

Level 4: Sharing your insecurities and quirks, for example, sharing that everything in your home has to be super organized, sharing that you have a fear of failure and others.

So, in the early stages of a relationship, we tend to share at level 1 and sometimes level 2. But in order to have a meaningful connection, we need to advance to levels 3 and 4.

One way to work toward deepening your relationships through conversation and mutual self-disclosure is to follow the guidelines below:

1. Determine what level you are currently at with the person you'd like to deepen your relationship with.

2. Make a goal to start sharing more about yourself at that level and observe the other person's reaction.

For example, say you are at level 1 with someone, and you want to move the relationship to level 2. You could come up with a goal that the next time you meet up with the person, you will share at least five new facts about yourself with them and see how they respond. Are they sharing back? And are they interested, curious, and accepting of what you have to say? If so, then perhaps in the following meet-up, you can try to share one thing from level 2 and see how that goes. If their response is favorable again, then you can slowly start to share more and more at level 2 until it feels comfortable enough to set a new goal and start sharing at the next level, and so on.

You will probably remain at one level for some time—there is no need to rush to move to the next level. Rather stay at one level until you feel completely comfortable moving on to the next.

What if you'd like to share more about yourself with someone, but you still have doubts?

Well, there are a couple of questions you can use to help guide you in whether to leap to share and be vulnerable or not.

1.) Ask yourself what your purpose is behind wanting to share with the other person?

For example, do you want to share because you think it will create a deeper connection with this person, or do you want to share because you feel an urgency to move the relationship along?

It is important to understand your motivation for wanting to share, as this will help you answer the question of whether you are sharing appropriately or not.

What often happens is that people either overshare or undershare. When you overshare, you tend to share too much too soon, and this can leave you feeling exposed and vulnerable if enough trust has not yet been built. When you undershare or don't share enough, the relationship becomes stagnant because the connection can't move forward.

So think about why you want to share and whether the relationship is stable and emotionally safe enough to take the risk.

Another question to ask yourself is how would what you'd like to share create more closeness between you and the other person?

For example, will you sharing this information with the other person help them understand you better? Maybe you'd like them to know that you got into yoga because you were struggling with anxiety, and it helped you to de-stress.

Or maybe the other person has shared something with you, and you'd like to share a similar story to show that you understand and can relate. For example, maybe the other person has told you that they have trouble sleeping, and you have experienced this in the past too. You might want to share this with them and tell them what helped you was to drink chamomile tea before bed.

In both of these cases, what you share may have the potential to bring you and the other person closer because what you have shared either helps them know you better or helps them feel related to and supported by you.

A third question to ask yourself is whether the relationship is secure and emotionally safe enough for you to feel comfortable being vulnerable with the other person. Have there been some mutual self-disclosures already, and when you have disclosed something to the other person, have they responded warmly back to you?

A fourth question to ask would be a question about your feelings, specifically how you feel as you think about opening up and sharing this information with the other person?

Our gut feeling or intuition is usually quite accurate, so tune into this and notice what it's telling you. Do you feel nervous about sharing, and is it nervous dread or nervous excitement? Or are you feeling something completely different, like peace? It can be a bit nerve-wracking to share more about yourself, but if a good foundation has been built up between you and the other person, sharing should be a positive experience when you get past the initial fear.

A final question to ask yourself is how you hope the other person may respond and whether you are prepared for the person's response going either way—that is, in either a positive or negative direction. Asking this question is helpful because it lets you know whether you can accept either response and how to prepare yourself for the less favorable one.

After going through this final chapter, you should now feel confident not just in how to connect with people on a superficial level alone but also in how you can start to grow and deepen your connections. It's great to be able to talk to anyone and everyone, but many self-help books do not give any guidance on what to do next in terms of maintaining the new connections you make. In saying this, we hope you have found this to be a useful and valuable addition.

Chapter 8 Key Takeaways:

- ✓ Connections can be sustained by knowing how to talk to people and knowing what to talk about.

- ✓ To build meaningful connections, empathetic communication is required.

- ✓ Empathy can be demonstrated by practicing attentive listening skills when engaged in conversation with others.

- ✓ Mutual self-disclosure that moves from shallow to deeper conversation topics brings people closer together.

Chapter 9

Tips & Tricks

Do you feel overwhelmed by everything you have read so far?

Relax! Communicating effectively will become much easier with practice.

We wanted to give you a solid knowledge base with this book. Therefore, it is very detailed. Each chapter contains practical suggestions to help with specific communication challenges. The chapters have been organized in such a way that you can easily go back to a skill you may be struggling or stuck with and re-check your understanding of its basic principles.

But perhaps now you are thinking: "This is too complicated for me. I will never master all these skills and remember all these details."

Perhaps you are afraid that once you are in a real-life situation, all you have learned in these pages will evaporate from your mind, and you will find yourself as shy, awkward, and communication-impaired as ever.

We have kept something for this final chapter that will dispel your fears.

Remember the title of Chapter 1? Communication Skills Are a Necessity? The reason is that we humans are social beings, and we need to connect to our fellow humans not only for practical reasons but also to be happy.

Here is why you will love putting the recommendations of this book into practice: the results will make you happy!

Think of human beings as a source of constant surprise and excitement.

Sometimes there can be unpleasant surprises, but these negative situations can be handled, as explained in Chapter 7. Worst-case scenario: you can walk away if a situation with a specific person is beyond repair . . . knowing you will find a better opportunity with someone else!

That said, most human interactions will give you something positive once you put in a little effort to learn the skills. And never forget what we told you at the beginning: communication skills *can* be learned!

When you approach a new person, see him or her as a treasure chest: they have all sorts of interesting things they will share with you after you break the ice using the skills we have taught you in this book. Precious knowledge, interesting life experiences, fun things to do together, new business ventures . . . the list of all benefits we get from being in a good relationship with others is very long.

And there is one secret we have kept for you to tie it all together. Ready?

Human relationships are life energy

When we spend time with others, and our interactions are positive, it fulfills one of our deepest human needs: to feel a sense of belonging and acceptance from others.

We crave human connection on a soul level. That's why we feel so energized after we have fed this craving with, for example, a really great conversation, an amazing first date, or a successful business meeting. Even introverts who tend to get drained from too much social interaction are energized by good quality interactions with others.

What sets good quality interactions apart is attention.

We have already described Attentive Listening in Chapter 8. Now we can go a step forward and give you some more insight into what attention means to us.

We need the attention of our fellow beings. It literally nourishes us—emotionally. This is why communication is so vital.

When we are communicating healthily, we are giving each other attention. You have learned about being authentic in Chapter 2, about approaching people openly in Chapter 3, and about empathy in Chapter 8.

Now we are disclosing this great secret to you to tie it all together: attention is, in a way, the life energy we need to thrive. The feeling of being energized from positive interaction with your fellow humans is not an illusion; it is very real. It comes from the positive emotions triggered by successful communication.

Emotions are connected to the body. Many subtle threads cause physical reactions in your body, starting from your emotions. Remember what you learned about body language in Chapter 5? Here you have one more reason why we humans are so sensitive to body language: we are passing something to each other when we communicate, and we feel it in our bodies.

And this is your real "prize" for using the tools we provide you with in this book: a source of life energy and happiness that can never run dry.

This is the secret of communication: when you learn the skills, you can nurture your fellow human beings with healthy communication, and they will nurture you.

Avoid negative communication for the same reason: it drains human beings and makes them feel bad.

Now go out and enjoy!

Here is a final little gift for you: a series of quick tips to reinforce what you have learned so far.

1) **Smile!**

A smile can melt ice and hearts . . . but only if it is sincere. People will feel it by instinct if you are acting. Or if you are forcing it.

How can you produce a sincere smile? If you are in the mindset of being curious and honestly interested in people, smiling will come naturally to you.

When any stranger is a possible new friend or at least an interesting acquaintance, you will be relaxed, and smiling will happen spontaneously. Just when needed and just as much as needed. Your instinct will take care of it.

2) **Listen!**

"Sometimes what a person needs is not a brilliant mind that speaks, but a patient heart that listens."

− Anonymous

Good communication is more about good listening than good talking. When you listen to someone, you are giving them attention. And they will feel it, physically! Remember? Attention is life energy.

Here too, people will feel it if you fake it. If you are just pretending to listen but really just waiting for them to finish so you can do your talking, they will know.

Developing an honest curiosity about your fellow humans is what does the trick in this case too. Human beings are always interesting, and even the simplest person has some treasure waiting to be unlocked—if you are open to discovering it.

If you are a very self-centered person, it may take a little effort not to think of yourself all the time. Curiosity is your ally: repeat to yourself that people are interesting, and after a little practice, you will develop a real taste for listening to them with sincere attention. You will see their reaction to you improve dramatically!

3) **Ask questions**

When you are *really* listening to someone with honest curiosity, you will want to ask questions to get to know more about them.

There is no more apparent evidence that you are paying attention than asking questions. You are open toward the person in front of you, sincerely interested in what he or she has to say, and they will feel it.

Your instinct will guide you on how to keep it positive and respectful so that it will not feel like an interrogation or intruding on their privacy. What you have learned in Chapters 1 and 3 about reading social cues will support you in this.

Important: asking questions can also be a life-saver when you disagree with the view of the person you are having a conversation with. Trying to understand the other person's perspective before giving the wonders of your own work, as we learned in Chapter 8 about empathetic communication.

Being understanding can be challenging when you strongly disagree with someone, so turn your curiosity switch on in these situations. You will shift from trying to defeat the opponent's thesis to being interested in understanding it. Most often, the person will *feel* the energy shift and relax after a few more attempts at provoking you and open up.

Then you will be able to exchange opinions "without the sting." The conversation can end with both parties keeping to their beliefs but respecting each other and feeling they had a good and meaningful interaction.

4) **Keep eye contact**

Eye contact is very powerful. A person will feel your attention when you look him or her in the eyes, and vice versa.

You have learned how to use eye contact in an initial approach with a stranger in Chapter 3. When you have already moved past these first steps, you will find that eye contact is also fundamental in all aspects of human interaction.

But why is it so intense? There is a clue in the old saying: "The eyes are the window to the soul."

We *do* reveal a lot of ourselves through the eyes and see a lot of other human beings in theirs. This is why exchanging glances is already communication, even without words.

Do you have problems with establishing and maintaining eye contact? Too intense for you?

The solution is again in being honestly interested and curious about the person in front of you. And knowing that what is going on is an exchange of attention/life energy between you.

It will still be intense but being aware of the process will take the fear away. Enjoy the intensity instead of being scared by it.

You have learned how to be Proud of Who You Are in Chapter 2, so you can show yourself through your "soul's window," knowing that you are offering true value!

5) **Regenerate: take time for yourself**

Interaction with our fellow humans nurtures us but can also be tiring—even when it is positive.

Have you ever come home after a swell party with your friends or a successful business meeting and just collapsed on the bed and slept for twelve hours?

You don't need to wonder, *what's wrong with me?* Because the answer is: nothing! It is perfectly normal to be tired after some intense interaction with people and resting—regenerating is the healthy thing to do.

A healthy balance of "me time" and social time is one of the secrets to happiness.

The time you spend with yourself because you like it is not loneliness; it's "aloneness." Balance it wisely in your life with the time you spend with your fellow humans. You will discover that by doing so, one will enhance the quality of the other, and you will enjoy both much more.

Chapter 9 Key Takeaways:

- ✓ Be curious and honestly interested in human beings, and all the teachings in this book will fall into place and become easy to apply to your daily life.

- ✓ Communication is about giving attention to each other, and attention is life energy that nurtures us and makes us happy.

Discussion

The purpose of this book was to equip you with practical tips to help you become a better, more effective communicator.

Effective communication is a learned skill, so you will need to practice what we teach in this book regularly for the best results. You can't simply become a more effective communicator overnight, but we can guarantee that if you complete the activities in this book and if you return to the different strategies that we teach often enough, then you will attain your goal of becoming a more effective communicator. If you feel even a little more confident in approaching, talking to, and building better relationships with others, then this book has served its purpose!

All of the tips and strategies we shared in this book were based on our four primary precursors for effective communication.

Discussion

These precursors or components are at the very core of effective communication, and without having all of them working together, effective communication cannot happen. The four precursors we introduced were 'knowing and having confidence in oneself,' 'genuine care and concern for others,' 'being able to read social cues,' and 'adapting behavior, language, and content to one's audience.'

Once we had familiarized you with our model, we got straight into explaining and teaching you how to implement our first precursor, which was 'knowing and having confidence in oneself.' It was important to address this component from the start because, as we learned, when we wear a 'mask,' others perceive us as inauthentic; whereas if we know who we are, are confident in who we are, and present our true selves to others, this immediately makes us more likable and more relatable to others.

In the next part of the book, we focused on effective communication skills in the context of meeting new people. We covered everything from how to know if the person you'd like to approach is open to having a conversation, to conversation openers, to what to talk about, to how to keep a conversation going. We included a broad range of examples, from your personal to professional life.

Then, we dedicated a section to troubleshooting and looked at why conversations go wrong and what to do when this happens—whether you're dealing with someone you don't know very well or with a close family member or friend.

Finally, in the last part of the book, we went into what kind of communication is needed to build relationships and move relationships to the 'next level,' as well as gave steps on how to practice this type of communication.

This book is your very own comprehensive guide. You can continually return to it to refresh the skills needed to communicate with people more effectively. Whether you're looking to meet new people, need help communicating better in your professional life, or want to deepen your existing connections, we have covered it all.

Please Leave Us a Review :)

We would love to hear some feedback from you! Whenever you buy the book, hit us up with a review and a few words letting us know what you thought about the book, what you liked, and what you think we could do better.

We're only human beings doing what we love, but we're always striving to be better and to give you the best experience we can! We also love hearing all the amazing ways these books help you see life in a different way, so let us know and inspire us to keep going!

Leave a review on Amazon US here.

Leave a review on Amazon UK here.

References

Altman, S. (n.d.). Retrieved from https://www.allgreatquotes.com/quote-405784/.

Body Language, Posture, and Proximity. Retrieved from https://www.skillsyouneed.com/ips/body-language.html#:~:text=In%20an%20open%20posture%2C%20you,might%20imply%20discomfort%20or%20disinterest.

Brown, B. (n.d.). Retrieved from https://www.goodreads.com/quotes/10511718-authenticity-is-the-daily-practice-of-letting-go-of-who.

Bulkeley, G. (1692). Retrieved from https://www.gingersoftware.com/content/phrases/actions-speak-louder-than-words/.

Cherry, K. (2022, February 14). *Maslow's Hierarchy of Needs.* Verywellmind. Retrieved from https://www.verywellmind.com/what-is-maslows-hierarchy-of-needs-4136760.

Cherry, K. (2020, October 12). *The Basics of Prosocial Behavior.* Verywellmind. Retrieved from https://www.verywellmind.com/what-is-prosocial-behavior-2795479.

References

Cuncic, A. (2021, May 26). *What is Radical Acceptance?* Verywellmind. Retrieved from https://www.verywellmind.com/what-is-radical-acceptance-5120614.

Doweches-Wheeler, J. (n.d.). *How Core Values Help you Find your Purpose.* Bright Space Coaching. Retrieved from https://www.brightspacecoaching.com/blog/2020/5/10/how-core-values-help-you-find-your-purpose.

Doyle, A. (2022, February 26). *Conflict Resolution: Definition, Process, Skills, Examples.* Retrieved from https://www.thebalancecareers.com/conflict-resolutions-skills-2063739.

Economy, P. (n.d.). *18 Ways to Send the Right Message with Body Language.* Retrieved from https://www.inc.com/peter-economy/18-ways-to-make-your-body-talk-the-language-of-success.html.

English Standard Version Bible. (2001). ESV Online. Retrieved from: https://esv.literalword.com/.

Faleti, Y. (2017, July 18). *The Importance of Effective Communication.* Stevenson University Online. Retrieved from https://www.stevenson.edu/online/about-us/news/importance-effective-communication#:~:text=By%20delivering%20messages%20clearly%2C%20there,resolved%20in%20a%20respectful%20manner.

Hawthorne, H., & Lowenbraun, N. (n.d.). *10 Ways to Communicate with Empathy & Authority in Times of Crisis.* Retrieved from https://www.duarte.com/presentation-skills-resources/important-communicate-empathy-authority-times-crisis/.

Hishaw, A. (2020, October 5). *Seven Seconds to Make a First Impression - Make it Count!* Retrieved from https://blog.thecenterforsalesstrategy.com/seven-seconds-to-make-a-first-impression#:~:text=Our%20brains%20make%20a%20thousand,likable%2C%20trustworthy%2C%20and%20competent.

Lampros, J. (2014, August 26). *Socializing, not Social Media, is an Essential Human Need*. Standard-Examiner. Retrieved from https://www.standard.net/lifestyle/health/2014/aug/26/socializing-not-social-media-is-an-essential-human-need/.

Lama, D. (n.d.). Retrieved from https://www.azquotes.com/quote/1401369#:~:text=approach%20others...-,Basically%2C%20therefore%2C%20we%20should%20approach%20others%20openly%2C%20recognizing%20each,much%20difference%20between%20us%20all.

Lloyd, C. (2012, August 24). *Use the Ford Technique to make Small Talk Easier*. Retrieved from https://lifehacker.com/use-the-ford-technique-to-make-small-talk-easier-5937348.

McKay, B., & McKay, K. (2021, June 6). Social Briefing #7: How to Initiate Small Talk Using the ARE Method. Retrieved from https://www.artofmanliness.com/people/social-skills/social-briefing-7-initiate-small-talk-using-method/.

Merriam-Webster (n.d.). *Shy*. Retrieved from https://www.merriam-webster.com/dictionary/shy.

Powell, J. (n.d.). Retrieved from https://www.azquotes.com/quote/536785.

Raypole, C. (2020, September 1). *Positive Affirmations: Too Good to be True?* Healthline. Retrieved from https://www.healthline.com/health/mental-health/do-affirmations-work.

Robbins, A. (1986). *Unlimited Power: The New Science of Personal Achievement*. Simon & Schuster.

Sanders, T. (2006). *The Likeability Factor*. Currency.

Segal, J., Smith, M., Robinson, L., Boose, G. (2020). Nonverbal Communication and Body Language. Retrieved

References

https://www.helpguide.org/articles/relationships-communication/nonverbal-communication.htm.

Sheed, F.J. (n.d.). Retrieved from https://quotefancy.com/quote/1648472/Francis-Joseph-Sheed-One-way-to-prevent-conversation-from-being-boring-is-to-say-the.

Smith, D. (2020, February 18). *Nonverbal Communication: How Body Language & Nonverbal Cues are Key.* Lifesize. Retrieved from https://www.scribbr.com/apa-examples/bible/.

South University (2018, May 1). *Why Being Social is Good for You.* Retrieved from https://www.southuniversity.edu/news-and-blogs/2018/05/why-being-social-is-good-for-you.

Van Edwards, V. (n.d.). Mirroring Body Language: 4 Steps to Successfully Mirror Others. Retrieved from https://www.scienceofpeople.com/mirroring/.

You & Earth (n.d.). *What is a Precursor and How do they Work?* Retrieved from https://youthandearth.com/blogs/blog/what-are-precursors#:~:text=These%20precursors%20need%208%20essential,oats%2C%20nuts%2C%20and%20wheat.

Mindnatic

Printed in Great Britain
by Amazon